The Life Of Christ And The Death Of A Loved One

Crafting The Funeral Homily

Barbara G. Schmitz

CSS Publishing Company, Inc.
Lima, Ohio

THE LIFE OF CHRIST AND THE DEATH OF A LOVED ONE

Scripture quotations are from the *New Revised Standard Version of the Bible,* copyright 1989, by the Division of Christian Education of the National Council of the Churches of Christ in the USA. Used by permission.

Some scripture quotations are paraphrased by the author.

Library of Congress Cataloging-in-Publication Data

Schmitz, Barbara G., 1958-
    The life of Christ and the death of a loved one : crafting the funeral homily / Barbara G. Schmitz.
        p.   cm.
    ISBN 0-7880-0363-1
    1. Funeral sermons. 2. Church year sermons. 3. Sermons, American. 4. Episcopal Church — Sermons. 5. Anglican Communion — Sermons. 6. Topical preaching. I. Title.
    BV4275.S36   1995
    252'.1—dc20   94-24350
                                                                                CIP

This book is available in the following formats, listed by ISBN:
0-7880-0363-1 Book
0-7880-0364-X IBM 3 1/2 computer disk
0-7880-0365-8 IBM 3 1/2 book and disk package
0-7880-0366-6 Macintosh computer disk
0-7880-0367-4 Macintosh book and disk package
0-7880-0368-2 IBM 5 1/4 computer disk
0-7880-0369-0 IBM 5 1/4 book and disk package

PRINTED IN U.S.A.

Table Of Contents

Acknowledgements

I am grateful to my colleagues and friends who have encouraged me in my writing, as well as those who took the time to read the manuscript and suggest changes.

I am grateful to my parishioners, both those "at home in the body" and those "away from the body and at home with the Lord," who have provided time to write, opportunities to preach, and many of the ideas, stories, and memories which frame this book.

My thanks to Hope Publishing Company and The Church Hymnal Corporation for permission to use copyrighted texts.

Lastly, I am thankful for Cheryl, Mary Fran, and Martha, and for their unfailing support and encouragement in my priestly and writing endeavors.

Preface

I care about good preaching. I think most pastors do. Unfortunately, we get swept up in many other activities and easily lose sight of one of our primary tasks and responsibilities — reaching people with the Good News. This is especially true when it comes to giving a funeral homily.

This book is offered in the hope that it will fill a real gap: to help pastors craft, in the short time available, a funeral sermon that is individualized, theological, meaningful, and evangelistic. I trust it will be an indispensable tool for both new pastors as well as seasoned pastors looking for some fresh ideas and new approaches.

It is offered in the spirit of this prayer from the service of the institution of a pastor:

> *In preaching, O God, give me readiness of thought and expression, and grant that, by the clearness and brightness of your holy Word, all the world may be drawn into your blessed kingdom. All this I ask for the sake of your Son our Savior Jesus Christ. Amen.*
> *(Book of Common Prayer, p. 563)*

Barbara G. Schmitz
Ascension Day, 1994
Hamtramck, Michigan

Note To The Reader

How To Use This Book

This book is in two parts. The first part addresses the actual art and task of crafting a funeral homily. "The Challenge Of The Funeral Homily" begins by describing the particular challenges that a funeral homily presents. "The Life Of Christ And The Death Of A Loved One" gives the theological rationale for a liturgical approach to the task, and "Crafting The Funeral Homily" outlines a step-by-step description of how to craft the funeral homily.

The second part consists of sermons I have written using this approach. I trust they will illustrate the method as well as give readers some starting points for constructing their own sermons based on the liturgical year.

Each sermon lists suggested Scripture passages to be read during the funeral service prior to the homily. The Scriptures suggested are either used directly in the homily text, or parallel the text in some way. It is common to have one reading from the Old Testament, a Psalm, a reading from the New Testament, another Psalm (frequently the traditional version of Psalm 23), and a reading from one of the Gospels. In order not to clog the text of the homily, I have omitted Scripture references in the text itself when the source is one of the suggested readings. A list of Scriptures especially appropriate for funeral services is found in the appendix.

Canticles and music which highlight the homily themes are also noted at the beginning of each homily. They are intended to help the reader in putting together the funeral service. The full texts of the suggested canticles are found in the appendix. All the hymns quoted and suggested may be found in the Episcopal hymnbook, *The Hymnal 1982*. All the texts of the hymns quoted are in the public domain unless noted otherwise.

9

The following abbreviations and resources are used:

N. — insert the deceased's name

BCP — Book of Common Prayer (the Episcopal Church Prayer Book)

The Hymnal 1982 — refers to the Hymnal authorized for use by the Episcopal Church. The number of the hymn follows.

This book reflects my Episcopal roots and was originally written with my Episcopal colleagues in mind. I trust that clergy from other denominations will make whatever adjustments are necessary to accommodate their liturgy and circumstances.

Part 1

Crafting Homilies

The Challenge Of
The Funeral Homily

The phone rings. A death has occurred. The family of the deceased asks us to conduct the funeral service. As pastors, we now have before us the task of writing a funeral homily. For some of us, it may be an overwhelming task. It may well be one of the most difficult moments we face in our pastoral ministry.

To begin, we may not even know the deceased. It is frequently the case that we are asked to do a funeral service for a person we have never met, either because he or she was an inactive member of the church, or simply because the non-churched family of the deceased asked the funeral director to try to get a pastor from a particular denomination, and we happened to be called.

So the first challenge is that we often don't even know the person we are burying. We may not know the family, or even expect to see them again. What kind of homily is appropriate to preach?

The opposite problem may also occur: we know the deceased all too well! We wince at the mere thought of saying something nice about the dearly departed. Will we gloss over the obvious? What does an individualized sermon require of the preacher?

The second challenge is to be theological. We are aware that those attending the service and hearing the homily will not be the "usual crowd." Many may not be Christians. A few may not be at all interested in hearing anything remotely spiritual or religious. They are simply there to do what is called "paying last respects." At best, they may have some interest or curiosity in the Christian faith; at worst, they are there merely to carry out the deceased's last wishes. In many cases, we cannot assume that those attending the service have had much exposure to the Scriptures or the Christian faith.

The third challenge is to say something that will be meaningful, helpful, and pastoral. That means we've got to dig deep inside ourselves for what we really believe about death and resurrection and eternal life. Integrity demands that we not sidestep hard questions.

The fourth challenge is to be an evangel of the Gospel. An evangelistic sermon proclaims Jesus Christ in such a way that others are drawn to follow him as their Lord and Savior. In some denominations, this means the Sunday sermon includes an altar call; in others it happens so subtly that it passes everyone by. What is the right amount of evangelistic thrust for a funeral homily?

A few years ago I conducted a funeral service for a young man who was not a professing Christian. The family, by and large, was not a churchgoing one. A handful of family members from the South had come up for the funeral. Not knowing the deceased or the family, I preached a rather non-descript, generic sermon. After the service, one of the uncles remarked to me, "Thank you for not preaching a 'hell, fire, and damnation' sermon. Where I come from, the Baptists are always preaching that stuff. But I really liked what you had to say." I lightheartedly replied, "Oh, I charge extra for fire and brimstone." The uncle smiled, laughed, and gave me a hug. We connected in a way we might have not been able to had I preached a more "assertively evangelical" sermon.

While I am not myself inclined to preach "fire and brimstone," and while I do not think a funeral service is the time for an "altar call," this incident did lead me to reflect later on whether the evangelistic moment of the funeral homily had been used to its full advantage. Was my homily appropriately evangelistic? That is, did it present the good news of Jesus Christ in such a way that others may be drawn to follow him as disciples?

These are the sorts of issues I struggled with in the first few years of my ministry. I scanned the booklists and Christian bookstores for some help on how to write a funeral homily, but there was not much to be found. Nor, to be truthful, had

I heard many funeral sermons that I thought were worth emulating.

Time gets the best of us, too. As pastors, we are already engaged in preparing the main Sunday sermon, in addition to a mid-week sermon or two. Taking a funeral service means preparing another homily on short notice — usually two or three days at the most, and in pastorally challenging situations where we may have stayed at the hospital long into the night, the funeral homily gets written in a state of exhaustion.

The challenges, the lack of good material, and time pressure are all what lead us, I believe, to fall into giving the non-homily known as "the eulogy," where instead of preaching the Gospel, we use the homily time to give a recap of "this is your life" on behalf of the deceased (usually supplied by the family, often a whitewash, and frequently lacking in anything overtly religious). I personally came to have a harder and harder time reading these "obituaries"; first of all because it sounded as if I knew the deceased, when often I didn't, and second because they frequently highlighted things I felt uncomfortable saying.

I continued to struggle with my funeral homilies until a former parishioner died, and I was asked to conduct a memorial service. I had never met the deceased, and I did not know anything about either the deceased or her family, except that at one time they were associated with the parish. At the time, I was working on my Sunday sermon. It was February, we were in the season of Epiphany, and I was preparing a sermon on Epiphany themes.

As I scrambled to prepare some kind of homily for the memorial service, I had a flash of insight. It occurred to me in one of those "a-ha" moments that those same Epiphany themes would make a good funeral homily. The resulting sermon was quite different from anything I had ever preached, but it had a kind of integrity about it that felt good to me.

A few months later I was asked to conduct the service for a deceased man who was not a professing Christian. We were in the thick of the Great Fifty Days of Easter season, and I

15

wrote a sermon on Easter themes. At that point, I had not even recognized that I had now preached two sermons rooted in the church's liturgical calendar.

A year and a half later, I attended a Roman Catholic funeral mass as a friend of the deceased's family. We were deep in the season of Advent, and the preacher delivered a wonderful sermon, weaving in Advent themes and Scripture appropriate for Advent throughout. That day, I began to realize the power of crafting funeral sermons based on the life of Christ and the liturgical year.

Since then, I have written and delivered funeral homilies using this concept. I look forward to writing my homily and delivering it, and find that my homilies now are individualized, theological, meaningful, pastoral, and evangelistic. There is an integrity about them that I did not always sense before.

Yes, there are still family members who press into my hand a list of the deceased's "vital facts," memberships, and accomplishments. I now kindly ask them if they, or another family member would like to deliver those remarks as an eulogy. I explain that I will be preaching from the Scripture, since it is a worship service, but that they are welcome to "give the eulogy" after my homily (or sometimes, before the service begins). This seems to work out just fine.

Preparing a funeral homily will always, I suspect, be challenging. But it need not be an overwhelming or frustrating task. It can be, rather, an enriching immersion into the liturgical year, Scripture, and the very core of the Christian faith. It may not be something we ever eagerly look forward to doing, but it can be a satisfying pastoral task. A step-by-step approach for crafting the funeral homily based on the liturgical year is presented in the next section.

The Life Of Christ And The Death Of A Loved One

"What is truly taking place in our lives is not determined by the random ups and downs of our personal and communal lives but rather by the events of Christ's life being realized among us in and through the church." (Henry Nouwen, *Sojourner's Magazine*, August, 1981, page 20).

During Advent, Christ is coming.

During Christmas, Christ is being born.

During Epiphany, Christ is being manifested.

During Lent, Christ is suffering.

During Holy Week, Christ is dying.

During the Great Fifty Days of Easter, Christ is risen and ascended.

During Pentecost, Christ is sending forth the Spirit.

"All other events," Nouwen continues, "personal, social, or political, derive their meaning from the Christ event."

If this is true, then all events in our lives, including the death of a loved one, take place within this "Christ event." It is only natural, then, that in preparing a funeral homily, we first ask the question, "Of what Christ event are we in the midst?" I am suggesting that one of the chief purposes of the funeral homily is to relate the church year and specific events in the life of Christ to the situation at hand: the death of a loved one.

Dietrich Bonhoeffer put it this way: "It is not that God is the spectator and sharer of our present life, howsoever important that is; but rather that we are the reverent listeners and participants in God's action in the sacred story, the history of Christ on earth" (*Life Together,* New York: Harper, 1954, p. 53). Bonhoeffer was talking about daily reading of the Bible, but his words also apply, I believe, to the task of writing a funeral homily.

Our task is not first to say something comforting (although that certainly is important) nor to give an eulogy, lauding the accomplishments of the deceased, but our first task is to ask, "Of what Christ/God/faith event are we in the midst?" which is to say, "At what point are we in the liturgical year?" I propose that that is an adequate, sufficient, and proper basis for building a funeral homily.

Of course, one way to answer that question (and always be correct) is to say, "Easter." A funeral is, first and foremost, a service of praise and worship in thanksgiving to God for the resurrection of Jesus Christ. So when a Christian dies, we bring out the paschal candle, the white vestments, the alleluias, the Easter songs, and for the space of an hour or so, it is Easter once again. The burial liturgy is without doubt an Easter liturgy. So I suggest that recognizing that the underlying base season is Easter, we further ask, "What liturgical season (Advent, Lent, Pentecost) is it? What liturgical themes particularly stand out?"

For example, Advent is traditionally the season of the four last things: judgment, death, hell, and heaven. Other Advent themes include preparation, waiting, hope, expectation, yearning, pregnancy, repentance. Some of these words immediately suggest themselves as funeral homily material. Some are, on the surface, less appropriate; all of them to some degree are fodder for the funeral homily. But this is the base, the foundation, the beginning of the task before us.

But shouldn't the funeral homily tell something of the person's life? Think about the other sacramental events for which we prepare and deliver sermons: baptism, confirmation, anointing of the sick, marriage, ordination. What is a proper focus of a sermon at each of those occasions? While referring in the homily to the person(s) about to be baptized is not unheard of, and while ordination sermons frequently have some kind of "charge" directly aimed at and referring to the ordinand, ordinarily the person involved in the sacrament is not the prime focus. Rather, the emphasis is on how the lives of the persons being baptized, married, or ordained help us tell our own stories as Christ's own more effectively. Likewise for a funeral homily.

But shouldn't we try to help grieving people feel better? No; neither is the focus of a funeral homily aimed at helping people to feel a certain way. Our prime purpose in a homily at a baptism or marriage or ordination is not to heighten the joy; the joy is already there in such heavy doses that it would be foolish to try to improve upon it with words. Nor would we write one sentence which would mitigate or attempt to decrease that joy. The homily on those great occasions pays little attention to what people might be feeling. Neither is a funeral homily first and foremost about trying to say some comforting, assuring words. In the course of the homily, hopefully that will happen; but it is not the primary thrust.

The first question, then, in crafting a funeral homily is, "Of what event in the life of Christ are we in the midst of celebrating?" The answer to that question forms an adequate, sufficient, and proper base for the funeral homily.

Crafting The Funeral Homily

Once we have identified the seasonal (liturgical) theme, the second step in crafting the homily is to try to grasp the key theological themes. At baptism, for example, we craft a sermon around the biblical themes of repentance, forgiveness, grace, adoption, covenant, and new birth. The sermon at the celebration of a marriage tries to capture the theological concepts of commitment, fidelity, and love.

If we try to do the same for a funeral homily, we only have to ask, "What is going on theologically at death and dying?" Some possible answers might include these sorts of theological concepts and words: life, heaven, sacrifice, presence, dwelling place, hope, freedom from bondage, "changed, not ended," resurrection, victory over death, Easter, dust, expectation, preparation, saints, eternity, judgment, purgatory, light, heavenly banquet, and so on.

The second step, then, is to combine the seasonal (liturgical) themes with appropriate funeral themes, to come up with an overarching theme for this funeral of this person at this time. For example, a funeral in Advent might suggest a funeral homily theme of preparation, hope, or expectation. What is known about the deceased (if anything) will hopefully help steer us in one direction or another as to what is a most appropriate theme.

We are ready, then, to begin composing the actual homily. The next question to ask is, what Scripture readings, what prayer book (liturgical) options, what music, and what prayers relate to, speak to, or otherwise address this theme?

The typical burial readings, including (in the Episcopal liturgy) 5 from the Old Testament, 10 Psalms, 6 from the New Testament, and 5 Gospel readings, are rich in the themes we have mentioned. There is no reason to strictly limit ourselves to them, however. For example, I used Romans 6:3-11 regarding baptism ("if we have been united with him in a death like his, we will certainly be united with him in a resurrection like his") at the funeral of an adult woman I had baptized less then a year before she died. The Roman Catholic lectionary includes Matthew 25:1-13 (the parable of the ten maidens) which is an excellent Gospel in the context of Advent, and Matthew 25:31-46, the story of the sheep and the goats, which has a more somber judgment theme, but which echoes the verse appropriate for funerals, "Come, O blessed of my Father."[1]

Secondly, the liturgy is rich in options that are not used to their fullest potential. For example, the alternate canticles in the Book of Common Prayer (the Nunc Dimittis, Pascha Nostrum, and Benedictus Dominus Deus) provide all kinds of rich material to weave into the fabric of the chosen theme. It is helpful to spend time reading through the funeral service, especially where options are provided (in the Book of Common Prayer, these include: opening anthem, collects on pages 493-494, the prayers on pages 496-497 and 503-505, offertory sentence, eucharistic prayer A,B,C,D; blessing/dismissal, commendation canticles). Choose those options which reinforce the theme of the homily.

Hymnals are also rich resources for the funeral homily. Various seasonal themes can be found in the Burial hymns, the Easter hymns, as well as the general hymns. For example, one could craft an entire funeral sermon around Psalm 84 and the hymn based on it, "How Lovely Is Thy Dwelling Place" (*The Hymnal 1982*, 517).

Lastly, select general prayers (in the Prayer Book, see pages 503-505), other collects and prayers from the funeral liturgy, or the prayers found in resources like J. B. Bernardin's *Burial*

---

[1] I might caution the reader that I am not proposing "theme preaching" that imposes a theme on a text of Scripture. But, having done our exegesis of the text first, and having noted appropriate themes and usages, we might appropriately select a particular Scripture text when constructing the homily.

Services. Try to match the theme, incorporating phrases and bits and pieces into the homily.

By this time, a wealth of material around a theme should be gathered; it is now a matter of working it all together around a verse or passage of Scripture, a hymn or phrase from the prayer book, around a collect, etc. At this point, if there are appropriate stories regarding the deceased that fit in well, this is the place to begin interlacing them into the homily.

Even where we have no prior knowledge of the deceased's life, a minimal amount of pastoral contact with the family prior to the funeral will suggest a story or incident which properly lends itself to the homily.

Whatever the season, theme, Scripture, prayers, hymns, and resources chosen, it is helpful to structure the content of the homily into four movements: a Christian understanding of grief (grieving as a normal, healthy, Christian response); gratitude for the life of the deceased; proclamation of the Word (the Christian faith rooted in the resurrection of Jesus Christ, as found in Holy Scripture); and an evangelistic thrust (an invitation to the bereaved to examine and grapple with their own lives). Looked at another way, the homily helps the bereaved to consider in turn the deceased, the Redeemer Jesus Christ, and the living of their lives.

I tend to take these up in the order given (I call them "the four 'G's": grief, gratitude, God, and grappling). My reasoning for usually beginning with a few words on the grieving process is simply that the bereaved are typically very open to hearing about grief. It is not something we talk about much in our society. For example, I often say that people have many ways of grieving, that that's okay, and then encourage them to take the time needed to do it. It is a simple, pastoral way to begin the homily and invite people into it.

In time, mourners will experience the grief giving way to gratitude. It is helpful to encourage the bereaved to give thanks (and thereby begin that process, if it has not already begun). People are usually eager to do this, and it teaches eucharist (thanksgiving) as a very important part of our faith, in a way the bereaved can all embrace.

The third movement is the proclamation of the Word, using the main Scripture or theological theme selected. I have a friend who calls this "preaching the comfort of Holy Scripture." I do not worry so much if it is comforting. I simply focus on preaching the Word, and leave whether it is comforting or challenging up to the hearer! Certainly the promise of eternal life to those who believe in Christ is comforting where the deceased professed and lived the faith. I presume it is not so comforting for others. Jesus did not hesitate to speak of judgment and other unpleasant things. My objective is to preach the truth of the Word of Scripture, and leave its effect to the hearer.

Lastly, it is always appropriate to invite the bereaved to see in this death an occasion to examine their own lives and grapple with the ultimate questions we all ask but which get lost in day-to-day living. Death has brought us face to face again with eternal questions. Let's ask them. A funeral homily may be the greatest opportunity to reach the lost that we regularly forfeit. When else do we have dozens, maybe even hundreds, of people listening to us who do not know Christ? They may not attend a worship service or hear a funeral homily again for months or years. We dare not forfeit that opportunity as ordained ministers and pastors who have promised to proclaim the Gospel of Jesus Christ.

By addressing grief, gratitude, God, and inviting the bereaved to grapple with the meaning of their lives, we address those things the bereaved came to the funeral expecting, perhaps even eager, to hear: something about the deceased, something about God and the Christian faith, and something about themselves. We will have used the homiletic moment well!

Part 2

Homilies

Sleepers, Wake!
A Funeral Homily For Advent

Matthew 25:1-13
Canticle: *Benedictus Dominus Deus*
Music: *Sleepers, Wake!*

One of the most powerful hymns I have ever experienced is the Advent hymn, "Sleepers, Wake!" It was written and composed by a pastor in Westphalia during an epidemic rage in which over 1,300 of his parishioners took ill and died.

As he stood by his flock, watching them collapse to the epidemic one after the other, he wrote "Sleepers, Wake!" It is nothing short of a wake-up call in the face of death: a summons to prepare for our death, and to be ready for the advent, the coming of Christ.

Listen to these words:

> *Sleepers, wake! A voice astounds us, the shout of rampart guards surround us: "Awake, Jerusalem, arise!" Midnight's peace their cry has broken, their urgent summons clearly spoken: "The time has come, O maidens wise! Rise up and give us light; the Bridegroom is in sight. Alleluia! Your lamps prepare and hasten there, that you the wedding feast may share."*
>
> *(The Hymnal 1982, 61)*[1]

"Thy time has come, O maidens wise." The end is here. Your lamps prepare. In the face of death, the pastor/songwriter urged his parishioners to wake up. Sleepers, wake! Are you prepared to meet Christ?

Are You Ready To Meet Christ?

We are, of course, in that season of the church year when we ask precisely that same question. We are in Advent, that season of waiting and watching, waking and preparing, getting ready to meet Christ once more on Christmas morn. Advent asks, are you prepared to meet Christ, not just as an infant in a manger, but as ruler of the universe? Are you able to join in verse three of the hymn,

> *Lamb of God, the heavens adore you; Let saints and angels sing before you . . . No eye has known the sight, no ear heard such delight: alleluia! Therefore we sing to greet our King, forever let our praises ring.*
> *(The Hymnal 1982, 61)*[1]

Sleepers, wake! Are you prepared to meet Christ?

That is the question the parishioners in Westphalia faced; it is the question that Advent asks every year; and, it is the question before us today, in this time of being saddened by the death of your loved one, N. Sleepers, wake up! Are you ready to meet Christ?

Ten Maidens

Jesus had some things to say about being prepared for that final day. In the 25th chapter of the Gospel according to Matthew, we read that the disciples said to Jesus, "Tell us when the end of the world will take place and what signs will accompany it."

Jesus, as he often did, replied with a story. He told a story about some young women who were ready to meet Christ, and some who were not. "The kingdom of heaven will be like this," he said. "Ten maidens took their lamps and went to meet the bridegroom."

Now, in Jesus' day, the maidens kept the bride company while the bridegroom negotiated the marriage with his future father-in-law. The five foolish maidens thought the negotiating would be over before dusk, so they didn't bother to bring along extra oil for their lamps. But the five wise maidens brought flasks of oil along just in case.

28

When the bridegroom was delayed in coming, all the maidens fell asleep. Suddenly the bridegroom's best man came shouting the good news: "Look! Here is the bridegroom! Come out to meet him! The time has come, O maidens wise!"

All the maidens hurriedly got up and began to light their lamps. The foolish ones, who had not brought enough oil, said to the wise maidens, "Rise up and give us light: the Bridegroom is in sight" *(The Hymnal 1982,* 61).[1]

The wise maidens refused. "Go buy some for yourself," they insisted. While they were off to find oil, the bridegroom arrived and the wise maidens joined him, going together into the wedding feast.

Later on that evening, as the festivities were really getting going, the foolish maidens returned from their search for oil. They knocked on the door and pleaded to come in: "Lord, Lord, open the door to us."

But the bridegroom replied, "Truly, I tell you, I do not know you." And Jesus concluded the story by saying, "Keep awake, therefore, for you know neither the day nor the hour."

Sleepers, Wake!

Sleepers, wake, indeed. We are, all of us, like the maidens waiting for the bridegroom to come: waiting, in these long days of December darkness, to greet Christ on Christmas morn. And more importantly, waiting, in the long shadows of our lives, for Christ's coming at the end of time.

One day the time will come for us, as it has come today for N. The question is, "Are we prepared to meet Christ?" Will we be like the wise maidens who were prepared, their extra stock of oil ready, awaiting the bridegroom's coming? Or will we be like the foolish maidens, who thought, "We do not have to be prepared. We can take care of things at the last minute. We will not worry about being ready when the bridegroom comes."

This season of Advent and this time of death both remind us:

> *The time has come, O maidens wise!*
> *Rise up and give us light; the Bridegroom is in sight,*
> *Alleluia!*
> *Your lamps shine and hasten there, that you the wedding*
> *feast may share.*   *(The Hymnal 1982,* 61)[1]

Sleepers, wake! The wise maidens who have longed for Christ's coming and who prepared for it will join the great throng in singing, as harps and cymbals swell the sound.

> *Twelve great pearls, the city's portals: through them we*
> *stream to join the immortals as we with joy God's throne*
> *surround.*
> *No eye has known the sight, no ear heard such delight:*
> *Alleluia!*
> *Therefore we sing to greet our King: forever let our*
> *praises ring.*   *(The Hymnal 1982,* 61)[1]

Sleepers, wake!
               Amen.

Death In The Midst Of Birth
A Funeral Homily For Christmas

1 Corinthians 15:20-26, 35-38, 42-44, 53-58
Canticle: *Nunc Dimittis*

There is probably no more difficult a time to mourn the loss of a loved one and join in the burial prayers than this. The twelve days of Christmas are for celebration, festivity, lightheartedness, merriment; a time to celebrate birth and God's love in sending Jesus to us. But for us this year, the twelve days of Christmas mean sorrow, loss, grief, and death. In the season of birth, we are in the season of death.

I'd like to share two personal memories with you, because they both have to do with Christmas and the placing side-by-side of birth and death. I was ordained a deacon in the month of June. My first Christmas I was at the Cathedral. The Bishop was going to celebrate the Christmas Eve service, his very last, as he planned to retire seven days later at the end of that year. I remember standing there and thinking what a strange moment in time that was, the Bishop celebrating his last Christmas Eucharist. After 30 years of ordained ministry, he was on his way out; and I, at my first Christmas Eucharist as a deacon, was just beginning ordained ministry.

As I stood reflecting on that moment, I remembered what a poet/priest once wrote when her husband died suddenly at a young age. At almost precisely that same time, a relative of hers, as I remember, perhaps her niece, was giving birth to a child. The priest suggested in her poem that maybe, just maybe, these two souls passed by one another in eternity, one coming into the world, and the other going out. Perhaps, she mused, they even greeted one another.

My other memory also involves a Christmas celebration, the December after I was ordained priest, when I celebrated at my first Christmas Eucharist. I was taken up in all the joy of celebrating Christ's birth as a newly ordained priest. But when I broke the bread and said, "Christ our Passover is sacrificed for us," the reality of Christ's death broke into my consciousness. The stark naked fact of Christ's death I was suddenly holding in my hands in the form of broken bread. Christmas and death . . . which one was more real? I remember feeling confused. Was it Christmas and celebration; or was it time for death and dying?

And that is where I suspect we are this morning . . . caught smack in the middle between celebrating the birth of Christ and mourning the death of N. . . . Which one is real for us?

I would like to suggest that both are real; our sanity depends on keeping *both* birth and death, celebration and grief, before us in three ways today.

First, we keep birth and death before us as we mourn the loss of our friend and loved one, N. There is probably not a more difficult time to do the work of grieving. Everyone else is celebrating and enjoying the festivities of the season; but we do not feel very merry. Well-meaning friends may try to cheer us up because they do not want us to be a damper on the holiday spirit. We don't know whether to stay home and grieve by ourselves, of go to the get-togethers we've been invited to and try to be cheerful. Christmas is not an easy time to do the work of remembering, crying, grieving, feeling sad. But I encourage you to do it anyway. Don't worry about what anybody else thinks. Take the time you need to grieve your loss.

Secondly, I can't help thinking about the mixed feelings God must have had at that very first Christmas. The Gospel of John tells us that in the beginning, the Word, Jesus, God's Son, was with God. But because we had fallen into sin, God loved the world so much that God sent Jesus to us. Think about that for a moment. Christmas, the celebration of Jesus' birth and coming into the world, was for God and Jesus, a separation, a breaking of the intimate communion and fellowship that they had shared, Father and Son, from before time.

And worse yet, the only way for Jesus and God to be restored to full fellowship would be through Jesus' death as a human being. It is Christmas that makes Easter possible; it is Christmas that makes Easter inevitable. What I am saying is that in every birth there is a death. In every death, there is a birth. So, in some way, it is actually quite appropriate to be gathered here for the service of the burial of the dead for N. in the very season in which we celebrate birth.

Believing that death is the gateway to birth and new life is not a new idea. Many years ago, Paul wrote to the Christians in Corinth:

> But someone will ask, "How are the dead raised?" Fool!
> What you sow does not come to life unless it dies . . .
> It is sown a physical body, it is raised a spiritual body.

Our physical death is the gateway of spiritual birth. So, if we have spiritual vision today, we will be able to recognize that death contains the seeds of birth. As we say in the eucharistic prayer, "Life is changed, not ended." True, we are here to mourn the end of the physical body, but also to celebrate the birth of a raised spiritual body.

Thirdly, this season of Christmas is an annual invitation to see beyond the festivities and celebrations which can so easily lose their true meaning, to see beyond to the true meaning of Christmas, which is found in Easter Day and Jesus' resurrection from the dead. In this season of birth, it is appropriate to ask ourselves if we are prepared for our own deaths. Are we in charity and love with our neighbors? Have we repented of our sins and turned to Jesus for our salvation? Are we in relationship to God? Are we living as those prepared to die? Will we die as those prepared to live eternally with Christ?

So in this season of birth now veiled by death, we are asked to do the uncomfortable:

> To mourn, although almost everybody else is celebrating;
> to see in death the gateway, the birth canal to new life;
> to examine our own lives, and ask ourselves if we are
>   living as those prepared to die.

That is a lot for the twelve short days of Christmas. But when our mortal bodies have put on immortality, then we will be able to say with Paul:

Death has been swallowed up in victory. Where, O death, is your victory? Where, O death, is your sting? But thanks be to God, who gives us the victory through our Lord Jesus Christ.

Amen.

Changed From Glory Into Glory
A Funeral Homily For Epiphany

Isaiah 61:1-3; Romans 8:14-19, 34-35, 37-39
Canticle: *Nunc Dimittis*
Music: *Love Divine, All Loves Excelling*

There is an old story about a fellow who was not very handsome at all. He fell in love with a young woman, but he was sure that she would not be interested in him. So with the help of a surgeon he had a special mask designed, a handsome mask that was then placed over his face. With this handsome new look, he easily won over the woman he loved and they were married. But many years later, she discovered the trick and asked him to remove it. When he peeled off the mask, what was underneath, but a handsome face! For, after all those years, his natural face had taken on the handsome contours of the mask. His face had been transformed into the likeness of the mask.

The Christian life, from baptism to death, is a journey of being changed, transformed, into the likeness of Jesus Christ. Charles Wesley, the great hymnwriter of the eighteenth century, put it this way:

> *Changed from glory into glory, till in heaven we take our place,*
> *till we cast our crowns before Thee, lost in wonder, love and praise.*
>
> ("Love Divine, All Loves Excelling,"
> *The Hymnal 1982,* 657)

What does it mean to undergo this transformation, to be changed from glory into glory? How does such a thing happen?

As Christians, we believe it begins in baptism. The moment that we put our whole trust in the grace and love of Jesus

35

Christ is the moment that we begin the transformation. From that moment on, we are sealed by the Holy Spirit and marked as Christ's own forever. It means that we are on the way, just as Jesus' baptism was the beginning of his life's mission.

Our transformation continues as we gradually understand our life's meaning to be about turning things upside down. It was shortly after his own baptism that Jesus returned to Nazareth, where he had been brought up. Jesus was beginning to get a picture of what God had in store for him to do. One day he went into the synagogue, and stood up to read the lesson. He opened the scroll to the prophet Isaiah and read:

> *The spirit of the Lord is upon me, because the Lord has anointed me; he has sent me to bring good news to the oppressed, to bind up the brokenhearted, to proclaim liberty to the captives, and release to the prisoners; to proclaim the year of the Lord's favor.*

Jesus finished the reading, rolled the scroll back up, and realized, in a flash, that the Scripture was about him. His ministry was about turning things upside down, so that prisoners would go free, and the brokenhearted would find comfort. As we begin to act on these things, as we minister to those who are captive, burdened, imprisoned, an amazing thing happens. We are transformed more and more into Christ's likeness.

As we mature in the Christian journey, we see the glory of God only dimly. Our knowledge is only partial. The changing from glory to glory reaches a new height when we enter into suffering. The difficult times of our life are the fires which refine us into purer disciples of Christ.

The purpose of our suffering is to unite us closer to Christ, and it works within us to transform us. "We suffer with him," writes Paul, "so that we may also be glorified with him." The apostle also comforts us with these words: "I consider," he says, "that the sufferings of this present time are not worth comparing with the glory about to be revealed to us."

Our transformation into Jesus' likeness continues with our own physical deaths. Death is our "transfiguration." Just as Jesus' glory was revealed upon the holy mountain, so we reach a new state of being changed into his likeness from glory to glory. We enter the home stretch.

We are here to acknowledge that death is not the end for the Christian, but it is in fact a cause for rejoicing. For the next stage of glory, the most important one yet, has been entered by one who dies in the Lord.

At last God's glory is seen face to face, in the face of God's son, Jesus Christ. Now we are ready for the final transformation. In the direct presence of God's love, we are changed into his likeness. Like the fellow who stripped off his mask to find a handsome face underneath, the Christian at death awakes to find the human mask stripped away, and what is underneath? A soul transformed into the likeness of Jesus Christ! From glory into glory is now finished. Our transfiguration, our transformation, is complete.

This glory which the dead in Christ enjoy today remains a future hope for us. We still await the day when we fall asleep, and wake up in Christ's likeness. This is the promise for those who love God: that from the day of our baptism, through our life's mission and sufferings, until the day of our death when we see God's glory face to face, God is changing us into Christ's likeness, from glory into glory, until our transformation is accomplished.

So whether living or dead, those in Christ are assured of this, and this is what we celebrate today: it is but a matter of time till we are

> *Changed from glory into glory; till in heaven we take our place, till we cast our crowns before [Him], lost in wonder, love and praise.*   *(The Hymnal 1982, 657)*

Amen.

You Now Have Set Your Servant Free

A Funeral Homily For The Feast Of The Presentation

Isaiah 25:6-9
Canticle: *Nunc Dimittis*

> *Lord, you now have set your servant free,*
> *to go in peace as you have promised;*
> *For these eyes of mine have seen the Savior,*
> *whom you have prepared for all the world to see:*
> *A light to enlighten the nations,*
> *and the glory of your people Israel.* (BCP p. 120)

There is a story in Holy Scripture about Jesus as a new-born infant, all of 40 days old. His parents, Mary and Joseph, took Jesus to the Temple to present him to God. According to an old Jewish custom, they offered an animal sacrifice of thanksgiving and dedication to God.

An odd thing then happened. A very old man named Simeon walked into the Temple, took the baby Jesus into his arms, and praised God saying, "Lord, you now have set your servant free, to go in peace as you have promised, for these eyes of mine have seen your salvation ..."

And then an even stranger thing happened: Simeon turned to Mary, the mother of Jesus, and said that Jesus would turn things topsy-turvy, and looking at Mary, he said: "And a sword will pierce your own soul, too."

This event in the Temple, as told by Luke, is known as the Presentation, which we celebrated a few days ago, and it offers much for us to reflect on this day as we gather for the burial office for our beloved friend N.

First, Simeon supposedly said to Mary: "A sword will pierce your own soul, too." That was perhaps Mary's first inkling that Jesus' death would occur before her own; that this new life which would bring joy to the world would also bring sorrow to her.

This mixing of joy and sorrow we call grief. N.'s life has brought joy to our lives; N.'s death is also like a sword piercing our own soul. So we feel grief today, because somebody we love and whose life enriched ours will no longer be with us in that same way.

I suspect that Mary went home from the Temple that day with mixed emotions: joy that her healthy newborn had gone to the Temple for the very first time; sorrow and confusion and frustration at the words of Simeon; and uncertainty about what sword would pierce her own soul.

In our grief, we too will go home today with mixed emotions. Sadness, sorrow, grief; wondering how we will get along from day to day, knowing things can't ever be quite the same. We will go with fear for the future. So take time to grieve. Take time to grieve in a way that is comforting for you; whether it's talking to others, or crying, or needing some time alone. But make sure you take the time to grieve.

Secondly, Mary and Joseph offered up their son to God with gratitude. They "presented" him; they dedicated him to God. That is what we do this morning. With open hands, we commend N. to God with gratitude for the life we have had the privilege of sharing.

What are the things about N. for which we are especially thankful? Talk about them; rejoice in them; remember them; celebrate them. Give thanks for all the goodness and courage which have passed from the life of N. into the lives of others. Give thanks for a life's task faithfully and honorably performed. Give thanks for N.'s sense of humor and love and affection and strengths. Keep gratitude alive.

Finally, in the story of the Presentation, we read that as Simeon picked up Jesus in his arms, he recognized the infant Jesus as the long-expected Messiah. And then the old man Simeon said to God, "You now have set your servant free, to go in peace as you have promised." Setting his eyes on Jesus, recognizing and embracing him as the Savior of the world,

God's servant Simeon was now ready to die — to go in peace, as he put it.

Can you say today that you have laid your eyes on the Messiah? Have you recognized in Jesus the Christ, the Messiah, the Savior of the world? A person who has seen Christ is no longer afraid to die, and can say with Simeon, "You now have set your servant free, to go in peace as you have promised . . ."

It is the confidence of those who believe in the Lord Christ and follow him that, just as Jesus was presented to God in the temple, one day at our death, we too will be presented to God.

> *May we be presented on that day with pure and clean hearts by Christ our Lord. All glory be to God, and to Christ our Lord, and to the Holy Spirit, now and forever. Amen.* (Collect for the Presentation, BCP, p. 239)

A Time To Die
A Funeral Homily For Lent

Ecclesiastes 3:1-11; Psalm 90:1-12; Romans 6:3-11
Canticle: *Pascha Nostrum*

> *For everything there is a season,*
> *and a time for every matter under heaven:*
> *a time to be born, and a time to die.*

These opening lines from the book of Ecclesiastes say that there is a season for everything. There is a time to be born. There is a time to die. Such a time it is, for we are in the season of Lent. And if ever there is a time that the Christian faith dwells on death, practices it, even celebrates it, surely it is this time of Lent.

Lent began on Ash Wednesday with those solemn words of death: "Remember that you are dust, and to dust you shall return."

And in the words of the Psalmist, "You turn us back to the dust and say, 'Go back, O child of earth.' "

We receive the ashes of Ash Wednesday as a sign of our mortality: a precursor of our own death and those final words: "Ashes to ashes, dust to dust."

Lent is also the traditional time of self-denial, of practicing "dying to self." By our giving up of chocolate, meat, television, and other things, we practice, in ever so small a way, our own inevitable death.

Lent culminates in Holy Week with the reading of Christ's passion, the story of his crucifixion, the tolling of the bells on Good Friday at his death. Then Holy Saturday — the day the church remembers Jesus in the tomb. Altars everywhere are stripped bare. Veils shroud the crosses in churches across the country. Lent and Holy Week bring us face to face with death.

If one could choose the hour of one's death, then surely Lent, filled with all the symbols of our mortality, would be the time to choose. For everything there is a proper season, a time; and Lent is truly the time to die.

Baptized Into Death

For the Christian, however, death has already happened. Death is a past event. What am I talking about? I am talking about baptism.

Our baptismal day is the day, according to the Christian faith, that we truly die and join Christ in his death.

Listen to what Paul says:

> *Do you not know that all of us who have been baptized into Christ Jesus were baptized into his death? We were buried therefore with him by baptism into death.*

When the sign of the cross is traced on a person's forehead at the time of baptism, that is the real moment of death. Again, Paul explains:

> *At baptism our old being (our life before baptism) was crucified with Christ; our old body of sin is destroyed ... For one who has died is freed from sin.*

So death is not a new experience for a Christian. We have experienced it in baptism, and we die over and over again in ashes, in Lent, Good Friday ... whenever we die to self.

Death And Resurrection

So we are here in this season of death because N. has died. But strangely enough, we believe that we are not here to preside over a death. Rather, as Christians we are here to celebrate resurrection.

44

There is a time to die, but there is also a time to live.

"For if we have been united with him in a death like his," Paul says, "we shall certainly be united with him in a resurrection like his."

Make no mistakes about it: we are here to celebrate not death, but resurrection! As we say at every celebration of the eucharist, "Christ our Passover has been sacrificed for us. Therefore, let us keep the feast. Alleluia."

Traditionally, the liturgy of the dead, this burial service, is an *Easter* liturgy. That is, it finds all its meaning in the resurrection of Jesus Christ. Today, therefore, is a joyful occasion: it is the celebration of a time to live in the midst of the season of death.

So, for the space of an hour, we put Lent, its purple vestments, its solemn liturgy, its penitential petitions aside. Make no mistake: we are here to celebrate resurrection. For an hour or so, it is Easter: we bring out the Paschal Easter candle. We put on white vestments, symbol of the resurrection. We proclaim the triple alleluias of the Great Fifty Days of Easter precisely because the season to die has been transformed by our Lord Jesus Christ into a season to live!

"For if we have died with Christ," writes Paul, "we believe that we shall also live with him." Therefore what we do today is gather to celebrate the season to live: to live eternally.

We come, then, to celebrate N.'s life. It is for the next hour a season of life. A season of celebration. A season of resurrection.

A Time To Grieve

All of this does not mean that we will not grieve, or mourn, or weep over our separation. The love that we have for N. brings sorrow. This is a time to weep, a time to mourn, a time to lose, as the author of Ecclesiastes described. A time to die in the season of death. Yes, we acknowledge and struggle to accept the pain of this loss.

In the days ahead we will look to God to support us in our grief, to help us live each day. I encourage you to claim the promise of the book of Lamentations, that

The steadfast love of the Lord never ceases, his mercies never come to an end; they are new every morning; great is [God's] faithfulness. (Lamentations 3:22-23)

Comfort and help is never more than a prayer away, and God invites us to call upon that strength daily.

Alleluia

It is true that we gather this morning in the season of death.

For we are mortal, formed of the earth, and to earth we shall return. For so did God ordain when creating us saying, "You are dust, and to dust you shall return." (BCP p. 499)

But for the Christian, it is also the season to live. Our brother [sister] has entered into the nearer presence of our Lord. We are here to celebrate the season of resurrection. "For if we have been united with him in a death like this, we shall certainly be united with him in a resurrection like his."

So it is in the midst of Lent, we celebrate Easter. In the midst of death, we celebrate life. In the midst of ashes and dust, we celebrate resurrection. In the midst of sorrow we shout with joy this triple Easter alleluia:

Yes, all of us go down to the dust, yet even at the grave we make our song: (BCP p. 499)

Alleluia!
Alleluia!
Alleluia!
Amen.

All Glory, Laud, And Honor
A Funeral Homily
For Palm Sunday

Revelation 7:9-17

We are at that time of year when we observe Palm Sunday, the holy day which ushers in the awesome events of Holy Week. This is the day that Jesus rode upon a simple animal and entered the holy city of Jerusalem accompanied by shouts of acclamation. He was proclaimed as King of kings by those who spread their garments and branches of palm along his way. Today Jesus is hailed as King, but before the week is out, Jesus will be crucified on a cross.

In our churches across this land and around the world, Christians gather to reenact that holy event. We gather the green, supple, freshly cut palm branches to be blessed and distributed. Gladly waving the branches of palm, we process into the church singing "All glory, laud, and honor" to Christ, our Redeemer King (*The Hymnal 1982,* 154, 155). Upon our lips are words of praise. We hail Jesus as *our* king; the branches are signs of victory.

All this is very close to the picture we are given in the seventh chapter of Revelation (or visions) of what heaven is like.

In Revelation chapter 7 we read:

> *After this, I looked, and there was a great multitude that no one could count, from every nation, from all tribes and peoples and languages, standing before the throne and before the Lamb, robed in white, with palm branches in their hands ....*

The vision reveals that those who have died in the Lord, those who have stood firm to the end, are in God's presence.

47

Heaven is described as a great multinational gathering of people from every corner of the earth. It is a summit of epic proportions. Joining with people from all over the world who have trusted in Christ, they stand before the throne of God. They are drenched in God's very presence.

They are dressed in white, the color which symbolizes purity, the liturgical color of Christmas and Easter, of baptism, and ordination, and marriage; and therefore the color of saints and of burial. We have a foretaste of that being dressed in white today: the white pall over the coffin; the white veil over the communion vessels, the white stole and vestments.

In their hands, as in our hands this past Sunday, they carry palm branches, signs of the victory of Jesus' resurrection over the forces of destruction and death. Signs, too, of their own victory over death.

And what are they doing? Verse 10 reads:

> *They cry out in a loud voice, saying,*
> *"Salvation belongs to our God who is seated on the*
> *throne, and to the Lamb!"*

Those who stand before the throne acknowledge God and the Lamb as the ultimate source of salvation, of the total well-being of the people. Their salvation, their sense of wholeness, is not in their selves, not in their accomplishments, not in their money, not in their own goodness. Salvation, health, wholeness, and well-being come from and belong to God. God alone is the source of salvation.

The heavenly world responds to this with affirmation. The angels and elders and four living creatures say, "Yes, it is true that salvation belongs to God." They fall on their faces before the throne, and shout:

> *Amen! Blessing and glory and wisdom and thanksgiving*
> *and honor and power be to our God forever and ever!*
> *Amen.*

The echo of that heavenly chorus is heard on earth on Palm Sunday morning and every eucharist when we join our voices with angels and archangels and with all the company of heaven, singing: "All glory, laud, and honor, to thee Redeemer King!" and "Blessed is he who comes in the name of the Lord. Hosanna in the highest."

And there is another picture of heaven in this Revelation to John: those who have died in the Lord are in God's care. Listen:

> ... the one who is seated on the throne will shelter them. They will hunger no more, and thirst no more; the sun will not strike them, nor any scorching heat; for the Lamb at the center of the throne will be their shepherd, and he will guide them to springs of the water of life, and God will wipe away every tear from their eyes.

The picture of the end time is one of divine protection. Those with faith in Christ will never again know physical hardship, deprivation, or the cares of this world. Suffering, mourning, and tears will be no more. Christ will be at the center of their need, just as he is at the center of the throne.

In the face of death, in view of Revelation chapter 7, on Palm Sunday, this vision asserts eternal promises. It also raises some eternal questions: What palms are we waving? Whose praise are we singing? Before what thrones are we worshiping?

Those who worship Jesus Christ, the Lamb at the center of the throne, wave palm branches and process with song. When earthly Palm Sundays come to an end, we are promised that the procession will continue. And what a parade it will be, as all those who have trusted in Christ will join in one great voice:

> Blessing and glory and wisdom and thanksgiving and honor and power and might be to our God forever and ever!

49

. . . All glory, laud, and honor, to thee Redeemer, King.
. . . Hosanna in the highest! Blessed is he who comes in
the name of the Lord! Hosanna in the highest!

Amen.

Welcome To The Banquet
A Funeral Homily
For Maundy Thursday

Isaiah 25:6-9; Revelation 7:9-17

On the night before Jesus died, he gathered with his friends in an upper room. In that sacred space, three things happened that Christians have remembered and celebrated ever since.

Jesus Washes Our Feet

First, Jesus got up from the table. He took off his outer garment, and put on a towel. He put on the clothing of a servant. Scripture tells us that he could do this because "he knew that he had come from God and he was going to God." In other words, he knew who he was, and what he was about.

Then Jesus poured water into a wash basin and began, one by one, to wash the disciples' feet. When he got to Peter, Peter refused. "No," he said, "you're not going to wash my feet." Jesus insisted. Peter gave in.

A Japanese Christian named Koyama has suggested that when we die, Jesus will be with us as he was on this last night before he died. He will be waiting for us with a towel tied 'round his waist. He, the master, the ruler of the universe, will be on bended knee awaiting us. He will pour water into a basin. He will offer to wash our feet and wipe them with a towel. He will look deeply inside us.

Jesus will ask, "You've had a difficult journey, haven't you? You must be exhausted and dirty. Let me wash your hands and your feet. Let me be your servant" (borrowed from Mark Dyer in *Episcopal Life,* April, 1993).

51

Jesus Invites Us To Servanthood

The second thing that happened on this special night was that Jesus gave them a new commandment, a new mandate, which is why we call this "Maundy (or mandate) Thursday."

Jesus said to them, "If I, your Teacher, have washed your feet, you also ought to wash one another's feet. For I have set you an example, that you should do as I have done to you."

What does it mean to die and enter the nearer presence of our Savior? What does it mean to spend eternity in heaven? It means a place where people act as servants toward one another.

There is an old story about a fellow who visited a town. There was a large pot of stew, large enough to feed everyone in town, and the smell was delicious, but around the pot sat desperate, starving people. They all had spoons with very long handles which reached into the pot, but because the spoons were longer than their arms they couldn't get the stew into their mouths. So they went hungry.

Then the man visited another town, just like the first one, again with a pot of stew big enough to feed everyone. The people had the same long-handled spoons, but they were all well nourished, talking away, and very content. The fellow was confused. How could this be? "It's simple," said his guide, "for they have learned to feed one another" (borrowed from Brian Cavanaugh in *The Sower's Seeds,* page 33).

At our death, Jesus will invite us to live in love and servanthood toward one another for all eternity. That is what we call being in heaven.

Jesus Invites Us To The Banquet

The third thing that happened on that particular night was that Jesus took bread, gave thanks, broke it, and gave it to the disciples, saying, "This is my body, which is given for you."

Then he took the wine, gave thanks, and gave it to them saying, "This is my blood which is poured out for you."

During our lives on earth, we are nourished Sunday by Sunday with the body and blood of our Lord. At our death, Jesus will welcome us to our place at the table in the heavenly kingdom. "Come," he will say. "The banquet is ready."

And on that mountain the Lord of hosts will make for all peoples a feast of rich food, a feast of well-aged wines, of rich food filled with marrow, of well-aged wines strained clear.

And Jesus will take bread and wine, and bless it, and sit down to feast with us in the kingdom ... as it says in Revelation,

They will hunger no more, and thirst no more; the sun will not strike them, nor any scorching heat, and he will guide them to springs of the water of life ....

Christ Awaits Us

On this night, Jesus washed feet; he gave a new commandment to love one another; he fed them with his own body and blood. We who have been washed in baptism, lived in love, and been nourished by Christ's body and blood will find at our death that Christ awaits us. Christ washes our feet. Christ invites us to servanthood. And Christ will welcome us to heaven, saying, "Welcome to the banquet."
                    Amen.

Originally published in *The Word Is Life: An Anthology Of Funeral Meditations* by CSS Publishing Company, Inc., Lima, Ohio, 1994.

The Sting Of Death
A Funeral Homily
For Good Friday

1 Corinthians 15:20-26, 35-38, 42-44, 53-58

Perhaps it makes sense to state the obvious right up front. Here we are, gathered on this well-known day in the church year, Good Friday. This is the one day where the main thought on our minds is Jesus' death, the cross, his suffering and crucifixion. It's the day we Christians, near the end of Lent, and wearied by the 40 days of penitence, fasting, and self-denial, screw up our courage to stare right into the face of death.

And doubly so today. For N. whom we have known and loved has died. Does Good Friday have anything to say to us about the death of our friend and loved one? I believe it does.

You will remember that Jesus was not the only person who died on that first Good Friday. Luke tells us that two criminals were hung with Jesus, one to his right, and one to his left. One of the criminals said to Jesus: "Are you not the Christ? Save yourself and us!"

But the other criminal, a thief as tradition has it, talked back to him, saying: "Don't you fear God? You are under the same sentence of condemnation. We are only getting what we deserve, but this man Jesus, he has done nothing wrong." And turning his head toward Jesus, he said: "Jesus, remember me when you come into your kingdom." And Jesus replied, "Truly I tell you, today you will be with me in Paradise" (Luke 23:43).

So first of all today, we pray that as Christ promised paradise to the thief who repented, Christ would bring N. to the joys of heaven. "Today you will be with me in Paradise," Jesus said to the thief as they hung on crosses. Today. That is an incredible promise of Holy Scripture. Not somewhere down the road; not maybe; not if; not later; not "we'll see," but *today*. So *we* pray, asking Christ to bring N. to the joys of heaven as Christ promised the thief who hung on the cross: today.

Secondly, we are filled with gratitude. By your death, Lord Jesus, you took away the sting of death. As Paul wrote to the Corinthians:

> *Death has been swallowed up in victory. Where, O death, is your victory? Where, O death, is your sting? The sting of death is sin, and the power of sin is the law. But thanks be to God, who gives us the victory through our Lord Jesus Christ.*

Thanks be to God! That is the cry of Good Friday! That is why we dare to call this dark, bad, ugly, awful day *good*. Because on this good day, the sting of death is overcome, swallowed up, defeated. Death is no longer the final word. And so first of all we come to give thanks and praise and worship to the one who on this very day defeated the power of death. Thanks be to God, who gives us the victory through our Lord Jesus Christ! To him be glory for ever and ever!

Lastly, we have opportunity to reflect on the meaning of the events of Good Friday and what they mean to us. We have occasion to reflect anew upon our own lives.

Two sinners hung next to Jesus. Which one will we be at our death? Will we be the unrepentant sinner mocking the Messiah? Or will we confess our sinfulness, and turn to Christ and trust in him to be remembered? Good Friday demands that we ask that question; and our answer will affect eternity.

> *Let us pray: Lord Jesus Christ, by your death you took away the sting of death; Grant to us your servants so to follow in faith where you have led the way that at our deaths we may hear your voice: "Truly, I tell you, today you will be with me in Paradise."*

Amen.

Low In The Grave He Lay
A Funeral Homily
For Holy Saturday

Isaiah 25:6-9; Psalm 130; Romans 6:3-11; John 5:24-27

The past two days are two of the most solemn days in the Christian year. For yesterday, on Good Friday, Christians commemorated Jesus' death. Later that evening, Jesus' body was taken down from the cross, anointed with oil, and wrapped in linen. Then it was placed in the tomb, and a large rock rolled across to seal it.

Today, Holy Saturday, is the day that Jesus "lay low in the grave." Jesus' disciples were heartbroken. Their friend was gone: dead. No more miracles. No more healings. No more stories. No more sharing meals together.

The Jesus they knew would not walk again. They would not hear his voice. They had enjoyed the Last Supper with him two nights before, but now they will never eat with him again.

Holy Saturday is a solemn, grave occasion. In our churches, the altars are stripped bare. Crosses are draped in black. Today is the one day of the year that there is no celebration of the Holy Eucharist. It is true, death had done its worst: "Low in the grave he lay, Jesus my Lord."

Today N.'s body lies low in the grave. Today, Holy Saturday, our brother [sister] N., his [her] body having been cared for and dressed, will be laid in a tomb.

And we, his [her] friends and family, are full of grief and sorrow. We will miss our friend, his [her] voice, his [her] being with us, his [her] breaking bread with us.

Now, if that were the end of the story, it would be a sad story indeed. But Holy Saturday is not the last word.

The final word is not "low in the grave Jesus lay." The final word is "up from the grave he arose."

"The powers of death may have done their worst, but Christ their legions has dispersed." The *resurrection* of Jesus Christ *is* the final word; Good Friday and Holy Saturday are only the prelude to God's decisive action of Easter Day.

The Christian message is this: that resurrection is stronger than the grave; and God's love is stronger than death. And that is why today, even though we are still in Lent, our liturgy, the Burial Office, is not a Lenten service. It is an unmistakable Easter service. We put away the purple and black altar hangings and vestments and replace them with Easter white. We once again say our prayers with alleluias, double alleluias, and triple alleluias — Easter acclamations of triumph and resurrection.

Because Jesus was raised from the dead, death is not the final word for him, or for us. Jesus Christ destroyed death on Easter day, and brought life and immortality. And we who turn to Jesus Christ and put our whole trust in his grace and love will also be raised with him to eternal life.

The promise of God, writes Paul, is that we who have been buried with him in baptism will also live with Christ in the power of his resurrection.

Jesus lay low in the grave on Holy Saturday. But this same Jesus had said, "The hour is coming, and is now here, when the dead will hear the voice of the Son of God, and those who hear will live." The final word, the good news, is that Jesus arose. And we who hear his voice will live with him in the power of his resurrection.

Let us pray: O God, creator of heaven and earth: Grant that, as the crucified body of your Son was laid in the tomb and rested on this Holy Saturday, so may we await with him the coming of the third day, and rise with him to newness of life, who now lives and reigns with you and the Holy Spirit, one God, for ever and ever. Amen.
(Collect for Holy Saturday, BCP p. 283)

Alleluia, He Is Risen!
A Funeral Homily For The Great 50 Days Of Easter

Job 19:21-27a; Psalm 42:1-7; Romans 6:3-11;
John 11:21-27
Canticle: *Christ Is Risen* or *Pascha Nostrum*
Music: *He Is Risen, He Is Risen*

The liturgy for the dead, the Burial Office, for which we have come here today, is an *Easter* liturgy. And since we are in the midst of the Great Fifty Days of the Easter season, it is *doubly* an Easter liturgy.

Therefore, we call today a celebration: a celebration of Jesus' resurrection, and the celebration of the sure and certain hope of the resurrection to eternal life for those who trust in him.

Early in the nineteenth century, this joy of the resurrection captured Cecil Frances Alexander, a young poet and verse writer. He wrote an Easter poem for children, in simple words so that even children might understand. The first stanza of his poem is now the opening verse of a familiar Easter hymn:

> He is risen, he is risen,
> Tell it out with joyful voice,
> He has burst his three days' prison,
> Let the whole wide earth rejoice:
> death is conquered, we are free,
> Christ has won the victory.
>> ("He Is Risen, He Is Risen,"
>> *The Hymnal 1982,* 180).

These simple yet powerful words frame my message this day.

59

He Is Risen, He Is Risen

"He is risen, he is risen." Some years ago there was a large gathering in what was then known as the Soviet Union. A brilliant man spoke for 90 minutes on behalf of atheism, attempting to persuade the crowd to give up religion. When he was finished, a young Russian Orthodox priest approached the platform and asked if he could speak. The atheist speaker said, "Yes, but only for five minutes." The priest replied, "I won't need that much time."

The priest mounted the stage, stood before the microphone, and cried out in a clear voice, "Alleluia, Christ is risen!"

The response came back from the crowd: "The Lord is risen, indeed! Alleluia!"

The young priest turned to the atheist and said, "That is my speech. I need no more time."

Alleluia, Christ is Risen! The Lord is risen indeed, alleluia! That says it all, doesn't it? For here is the very center and meaning of our faith: Jesus Christ was raised from the dead. What difference does it make to us today?

It means that Jesus Christ destroyed death. The Book of Common Prayer says he "trampled down death by death" (BCP p. 500). Good Friday was not the last word. God raised Jesus up, and this is good news for us.

Paul says, "If we have died with him, we will be raised with him." Christ is risen — these three words change everything. This is what we gather here to celebrate: he is risen, he is risen.

Tell It Out With Joyful Voice

"Tell it out with joyful voice." Now, today a joyful voice seems far from us. Sorrow, sadness, and grief are close to our hearts. No doubt we can say with the author of Psalm 42:

Why are you so full of heaviness, O my soul,
and why are you so disquieted within me?

To grieve is not unchristian. Grieving is a natural expression of the care and love we have for one another, and of the sorrow we feel when parted by death.

But as Christians we are an Easter people. We believe that sorrow is not as strong as joy; death is not as strong as life; grief is not as strong as hope. And therefore we can shout out with joyful voice. And our shout is this:

He is risen, he is risen, tell it out with joyful voice.

He Has Burst His Three Days' Prison

"He has burst his three days' prison." The grave couldn't hold Christ.

He broke the bonds of death so that we might break forth from the prisons that hold us: prisons of fear, prisons of hatred, prisons of sin, prisons of sickness and death.

The power of Jesus' resurrection is stronger than any earthly prison that binds us, even death. When Jesus raised Lazarus from the dead, Jesus said to Lazarus' sister Martha, "I am the resurrection and the life. Those who believe in me, even though they die, will live, and everyone who lives and believes in me will never die. Do you believe this?"

Do *you* believe it? The invitation of Christ to Martha, and to us, is to believe it, to follow the one who in his person experienced resurrection, who is resurrection itself.

Martha responded, "Yes, Lord, I believe that you are the Messiah, the Son of God." Those who believe in and follow the resurrected one will also burst the prison of death. The grave can't hold them either.

Let The Whole Wide World Rejoice

Therefore, let the whole wide earth rejoice. Our faith allows us, encourages us; yes, even compels us to shout out with hope the words of Easter joy: Alleluia! In the words of the commendation, "All of us go down to the dust, yet even at the grave we make our song, alleluia! alleluia! alleluia!"

Job, in the midst of the worst suffering known to human beings, broke forth with joyful song when he wrote:

> *As for me, I know that my redeemer lives,*
> *and that at the last*
> *My redeemer will stand upon the earth.*
> *After my awakening, God will raise me up,*
> *and in my body I shall see God.*
> *I myself shall see, and my eyes shall behold God,*
> *who is my friend, and not a stranger.*

We are a people who grieve, but we are also a people who know hope and believe that God is with us; the same God who raised Jesus from the dead will also redeem us and bring us with joy into God's eternal presence.

Death Is Conquered, We Are Free, Christ Has Won The Victory

Finally, "Death is conquered, we are free, Christ has won the victory." When a Christian dies, the task of the church is nothing other than to affirm the resurrection. We are here today to remind each other and to tell those who do not know: In Jesus Christ, death is conquered. We are free. We are here to remember that Easter is not a day, one day that falls each spring. It is a season, it is the great time of celebration, the 50 days from Easter Day to Pentecost Day. And even more, Easter is an eternal truth, and a way of life.

We are meant by God to live every day with the joy and power of Easter Day: living out of love, not fear; living in joy, not sorrow. Because we are an Easter people; our grief is not forever, our sadness can not last.

Death is conquered, we are free, Christ has won the victory. That is our song today.

Therefore, in sure and certain hope of the resurrection, we proclaim the joyful verse:

He is risen, he is risen, tell it out with joyful voice.
He has burst his three days' prison; Let the whole wide earth rejoice.
Death is conquered, we are free, Christ has won the victory.   *(The Hymnal 1982, 180)*

Amen.

I Go To Prepare A Place For You

A Funeral Homily For Ascension Day Until Pentecost Day

Wisdom 3:1-5, 9; Psalm 139:1-17; John 14:1-6
Canticle: *Nunc Dimittis*

One of my favorite stories is the true story of a young couple who had a little girl and had just returned home from the hospital with a newborn baby boy. Their little girl kept begging to go into the nursery alone with her new sibling. The parents were afraid, as they had heard stories of children being jealous of newborn siblings, and thought she might want to harm the baby.

She kept asking to be alone with him, and they said no. "Why not?" she asked. "Well, why do you want to be with him?" they inquired. "What are you going to do?"

Finally the parents decided to try it. They put an intercom in the baby's room and listened in another room as the little girl went in to see her brother alone. The parents were ready to jump up and rush in if the girl began to hurt him. They put their ears to the intercom, and they heard the little girl tiptoe up to the crib. Then they heard the little girl whisper into her new brother's ear: "Quick. Tell me about God. I'm forgetting" (borrowed from Sophy Burnham in *Angel Letters*, p. 140.)

I like that story because it reminds us about something we tend to forget: that before we were born, we were in the presence of God. We were bathed in God's love. This is what the Psalmist affirmed when he wrote:

> *My body was not hidden from you, while I was being made in secret and woven in the depths of the earth! ... your eyes beheld my limbs ... they were fashioned day by day, when as yet there was none of them!*

Somehow God knew us before we were born, when we were nothing but the gleam in our parents' eyes.

And then, one by one, each of us left God's nearer presence and slowly began to take on human flesh in our mothers' wombs. Nine months in the womb and a few years of being helpless infants, and our memories of being in God's presence gradually faded away. By the time we were six or seven years old, those memories are all but extinguished. Occasionally we may have a flashback or some kind of spiritual experience in which we, for a brief moment, remember our life before we were born. We long to recapture that wonderful time. So the little girl in the story hoped her baby brother could revive some of those fading memories. "Tell me about God." she said, "I'm forgetting."

N., before he [she] was born into this world, was with God. He [she] looked upon God's face. He [she] bathed in God's presence and God's love. The time came for him [her] to become a member of a particular human family. For _____ years he [she] lived his [her] life on earth. On __(date)__ his [her] earthly life came to its finish. And we gather here and ask, what now? Is there more?

Yes. In the book of Wisdom, we read,

> *But the souls of the just are in God's hand, and torment shall not touch them. In the eyes of the foolish they seemed to be dead; their departure was reckoned as defeat, and their going from us as disaster. But they are at peace, . . . they have a sure hope of immortality . . .*

For the Christian who trusts in Christ, there is more to come: Again, from the book of Wisdom:

> *Those who have put their trust in him shall understand that he is true, and the faithful shall attend upon him in love; they are God's chosen, and grace and mercy shall be theirs.*

Jesus confirmed that there is "something more." In the 14th chapter of the Gospel of John, Jesus tells his disciples:

> *Do not let your hearts be troubled. Believe in God, believe also in me. In my Father's house there are many dwelling places. If it were not so, would I have told you that I go to prepare a place for you?*

"I go to prepare a place for you!" We celebrated this glorious truth on (last) Thursday, Ascension Day. Jesus, on the 40th day after his resurrection, stood talking to his disciples, when they saw him lifted up before their eyes and taken into a cloud. As we say in the Apostles' Creed, "He ascended into heaven, and is seated at the right hand of the Father."

But before Jesus took his place at his Father's side, he repeated these words in which generations of Christians have found assurance:

> *I go to prepare a place for you . . . . And if I go to prepare a place for you, I will come again and will take you to myself, so that where I am, there you may be also.*

Is death the end for a Christian? No, because Christ has promised to go before us and prepare a place for us. The purpose of Christ's ascension, which we celebrate now until the day of Pentecost on (next) Sunday, is to go ahead of us and prepare the way, so that where he is, there we might also be: back in God's loving, merciful presence. Ascension Day is about Christ's returning to heaven, but, you see, it is also about our return to God.

That is primarily why we gather here this morning: to celebrate the "sure hope of immortality," the return, for those who believe in Christ, to God's nearer presence, that presence we had for unknown years before our birth, when we were not yet; and, to celebrate that Christ has gone before us to prepare a place for us for all of eternity to come.

For those of us who remain, awaiting our own ascension, so to speak, to "the life of the world to come," this is also a time to reflect on our lives. We know that we have come from God, but do you know to whom you are returning? When the disciple Thomas said to Jesus, "Lord, we do not know where you are going, so how can we know the way?" Jesus replied: "I am the way, and the truth, and the life. No one comes to the Father but by me."

Do you get, from time to time, a glimpse of that wonderful existence you enjoyed before you were born? Moments in this life, filled with incredible love and unspeakable joy, are given to us to remind us of what it was like. God delights in giving us these moments of deep gratitude, joyful satisfaction, intimate love, and overwhelming awe to draw us to God and help us remember.

This is what Jesus meant when he said, "I am the way, the truth and the life." He was saying, follow me and open yourself to these experiences of joyful communion with my Father and with your brothers and sisters on earth. They are all around you, and I will help show them to you. And, when your earthly life is finished, I will have prepared a place for you. That same place you knew before you were born. That same place you experienced in your heart on earth. The place of being in my Father's presence, that where I am, you may also be, reigning in glory with us, as it was in the beginning, is now and ever shall be, until the end of the ages, world without end.

Amen.

Where Can I Go From Your Spirit?
A Funeral Homily For Pentecost

Psalm 139:1-17
Music: *Come, Gracious Spirit*

When Jesus preached his famous Sermon on the Mount, one of the things he said was, "Blessed are those who mourn, for they shall be comforted." Today, as we gather together to pray, we know firsthand the promise of Christ's words.

For it is natural, at such a time as this, to turn to the Holy Spirit, the Holy Comforter, as Jesus called the Spirit. We pray that the Spirit at this time of Pentecost may fall fresh on us again, to surround and protect and comfort us in our time of sorrow and loss, to quiet our fears, to dispel our doubts.

When you are cast down, not knowing where to turn, overcome with sorrow and grief, I encourage you to turn to the Holy Comforter, who will supply all your need, revive your hope, and increase your faith.

For our confidence is this: that the ever-present Spirit will not abandon the Christian in time of need. In Psalm 139, one of the most moving Psalms in all of Scripture, the Psalmist cries out, "Where can I go then from your Spirit? Where can I flee from your presence?"

The answer? Nowhere — "If I climb up to heaven, you are there; if I make the grave my bed, you are there also." The Spirit who has been with us from the time of our baptism, the Spirit who strengthens us in confirmation, the Spirit who pours out the abundance of blessing in holy matrimony, the same Spirit who leads us to confession and keeps us in eternal life, the Spirit who anoints us inwardly as we are outwardly anointed with oil during prayers for healing, this same Spirit does not abandon the Christian at the time of death:

Where can I go from your Spirit? If I climb up to heaven, you are there; if I make the bed my grave, you are there also. If I take the wings of the morning and dwell in the uttermost parts of the sea, even there your hand will lead me, and your right hand hold me fast.

Neither height nor depth nor distance, not joy, not grief, nor physical separation can wrest us from the ever-present Spirit.

The Spirit also knows us inside and out. Again, the Psalmist writes:

You have searched me out and known me, you know my sitting down and my rising up; you discern my thoughts from afar. You trace my journeys and my resting places and are acquainted with all my ways. Indeed, there is not a word on my lips, but you, O Lord, knew it altogether.

You see, the Spirit knows us, inside and out. Both our outward actions and our inward thoughts, our times of activity, and our times of rest, both our ways and our words.

"Even there your right hand will lead me and your right hand hold me fast." We are upheld in the Spirit's love and embrace.

Neither can darkness separate us from the Spirit. Not the darkness of night, nor the darkness of fear, nor the darkness of pain, nor the darkness of difficult circumstances:

For if I say, "Surely the darkness will cover me, and the light around me turn to night," Darkness is not dark to you; the night is as bright as the day; darkness and light to you are both alike.

We also rejoice in the Spirit who knew us before we were born, who created our inmost parts, who knit us together in our mother's womb. "I will thank you because I am marvelously made; your words are wonderful, and I know it full well."

The Psalmist gave thanks for the wonderful gift of being a human being. Today, we give thanks for the wonderful gift of N., his [her] life among us, his [her] love, wisdom, talents. It is right and proper to express our thanks over and over again to God for this unique person with whom we have had the privilege of knowing and sharing a part of our life.

And we rejoice because the One who made us in secret, weaving us together in the depths of the earth, fashioning us day by day, when we were not, will, after we die and return to the earth, keep working in us, keep fashioning us. We are not hidden from God after we die anymore than we were hidden from God before we were born.

The Spirit is with us today to comfort us in our sorrow.
The Spirit is ever present with us.
The Spirit knows us inside and out.
The Spirit is in us, working in us that which is perfect in God's sight.

In the words of Simon Browne:

So come, gracious Spirit, heavenly dove,
with light and comfort from above;
be thou our guardian, thou our guide
o'er every thought and step preside.

Lead us to Christ, the living way,
nor let us from his precepts stray;
lead us to holiness, the road
that we must take to dwell with God.

Lead us to heaven, that we may share
fullness of joy forever there;
lead us to God, our final rest,
to be with him forever blest.

("Come, Gracious Spirit,"
The Hymnal 1982, 512)

Amen.

I Bind Unto Myself Today
A Funeral Homily For Trinity

Job 19:21-27a; Psalm 139:1-17; John 11:21-27
Music: *I Bind Unto Myself Today*

> *Depart, O Christian soul, out of this world;*
> *In the Name of God the Father Almighty who*
>   *created you;*
> *In the Name of Jesus Christ who redeemed you;*
> *In the Name of the Holy Spirit who sanctifies you.*
> *May your rest be this day in peace,*
> *and your dwelling place in the Paradise of God.*
>   (BCP p. 464)

This prayer is most appropriate for today, as we just celebrated on Sunday what is known to Christians as Trinity Sunday. Trinity Sunday puts before us the mystery of the one God in three persons — Father, Son, and Holy Spirit.

As we gather here to mourn the death of N., this same mystery is held up before us today: the mystery of God the Creator, God the Redeemer, and God the Sanctifier. Let us come, then, once again, in this hour of loss and sadness, in the words of Cecil Frances Alexander, to "bind unto ourselves today the strong Name of the Trinity, by innovation of the same, the Three in One, and One in Three" ("I Bind Unto Myself Today," *The Hymnal 1982,* 370).

First, we affirm today God the Creator. As the Psalmist wrote:

> *For you yourself created my inmost parts;*
> *you knit me together in my mother's womb.*
> *I will thank you because I am marvelously made;*
> *your works are wonderful, and I know it well.*
> *My body was not hidden from you,*
> *while I was being made in secret*
> *and woven in the depths of the earth.*

73

Your eyes beheld my limbs, yet unfinished in the womb;
all of them were written in your book;
they were fashioned day by day,
when as yet there was none of them.

God knew us before time. God was present with us while we were being woven in the depths of the earth, and knit us together in our mother's womb. God loved us before we ever lived one day on this earth. Is this same Creator God present with us after our departure from this earth? How could it be otherwise?

As the Psalmist writes:

Where can I go from your Spirit?
where can I flee from your presence?
If I climb up to heaven, you are there;
if I make the grave my bed, you are there also.

God the Creator who was at work in us before we were born and during our life continues to be at work within us after our death.

We affirm also today God the Redeemer:

I bind this day to me forever, by power of faith,
Christ's incarnation; his baptism in the Jordan River;
his death on the cross for my salvation;
his bursting from the spiced tomb, his riding up
the heavenly way, his coming at the day of doom ...
(The Hymnal 1982, 370)

Do you remember Job, that poor fellow in the Old Testament who lost everything in one fell swoop — wife, family, home, health, and business? As he lay in grief and pain, he was still able to affirm his trust in God the Redeemer.

In chapter 19, Job speaks out in stirring words:

For I know that my Redeemer lives,
and that at the last he will stand upon the earth;
and after my skin has been thus destroyed,
then in my flesh I shall see God ...

Job believed in his redeemer.

In another time of distress, when Lazarus died, Jesus and Lazarus' sister Martha mourned. Jesus said to Martha, "I am the resurrection and the life. Those who believe in me, even though they die, will live, and everyone who lives and believes in me will never die. Do you believe this?

Do you believe this? Do you believe in God the Redeemer, Jesus Christ? Have you ever put your faith and trust in his grace and love? If you have not, I invite you to do so today, to bind unto yourself today the power of faith in the one Redeemer, Jesus Christ.

In death, as in life, you will be privileged to turn to Christ, and sing:

> *Christ be with me, Christ within me, Christ behind me,*
> *Christ before me, Christ beside me, Christ to win me,*
> *Christ to comfort and restore me.*
> *Christ beneath me, Christ above me, Christ in quiet,*
> *Christ in danger, Christ in hearts of all that love me,*
> *Christ in mouth of friend and stranger.*
> *(The Hymnal 1982, 370)*

Finally today, we affirm God the Sanctifier, the Holy Spirit who inspires and sustains and sanctifies and comforts us.

In your sorrow and grief, I invite you to look to the Holy Spirit for strength and comfort.

I invite you to bind unto yourself today

> *The power of God to hold and lead, his eye to watch,*
> *his might to stay, his ear to hearken to [your] need.*
> *(The Hymnal 1982, 370)*

God the Holy Spirit is with us to hold and embrace us, to carry us through this time of sadness. The Holy Spirit's eye is watching over us. The Holy Spirit is our source of strength and courage to face this day, and the next day, and the next, and the next. By the energy of the Holy Spirit, we are enabled to go on our way strengthened and without fear.

"His ear to hearken to my need." When you have no one to turn to, when you have grief and pain to pour out, turn to the Holy Spirit, whose ear is turned to you.

In death, as in life, we look to the Triune God who creates us, who redeems us, and who sustains us. It is with confidence and faith that we sing together the last verse of Alexander's hymn:

> *I bind unto myself the Name, the strong Name of the Trinity,*
> *by invocation of the same, the Three in One, and One in Three.*
> *Of whom all nature has creation, eternal Father, Spirit, Word:*
> *praise to the Lord of my salvation, salvation is of Christ the Lord.*
>
> *(The Hymnal 1982, 370)*

Amen.

A Sheep Of Your Own Flock
A Funeral Homily For The Season After Pentecost*

Psalm 121; Revelation 7:9-17; Psalm 23; John 10:11-16

No two ways about it, it has been a difficult few days, and we are in a difficult time. N., who has been part of our lives for so long, whom we have come to know and love and care for deeply, has died. We wish it weren't so. We wonder how we can go on without him [her]. We have unanswered questions. We know fear, and grief, and sorrow all rolled into one.

Many years ago, there was another person who had some of these same feelings. Not sure where to turn. Scared to death. Heartbroken. A shepherd by occupation, he spent his days corralling his sheep, keeping them fed, keeping them moving, untangling them from prickly bushes, rescuing them from steep ledges.

Perhaps it was in a moment of trouble and perplexion that the shepherd David looked to God for help and consolation. And he wrote down these words, probably some of the most well-known words in all the Bible:

The Lord is my shepherd; I shall not want.
He maketh me to lie down in green pastures;
he leadeth me beside the still waters.
He restoreth my soul; he leadeth me in the
paths of righteousness for his Name's sake.

Yea, though I walk through the valley of the shadow of death, I will fear no evil; for thou art with me, thy rod and thy staff, they comfort me.

Thou preparest a table before me in the presence of mine enemies; thou anointest my head with oil; my cup runneth over.

77

Surely goodness and mercy shall follow me all the days of my life, and I will dwell in the house of the Lord for ever.

"The Lord is my shepherd." These words were of great comfort to the shepherd David, and thousands upon thousands have likewise found comfort in these words. What does the shepherd do when the sheep are hurting? The good shepherd guides, protects, nurtures, and comforts the sheep. That is what God does for us in our time of trouble.

Yea, though I walk through the valley of death, I will fear no evil, for thou art with me. The promise of Scripture is that God is with us. God is with us.

God also watches over us. In another Psalm, the author asks, "From where is my help to come?" And then he answers his own question: "My help comes from the Lord, because the Lord is the one who watches over you" (Psalm 121). Is that not the chief job description of a shepherd? A shepherd is like a lifeguard, whose eyes are constantly scanning the water, peeled for signs of danger. God watches over us. But unlike a human shepherd or lifeguard, who needs periods of rest and refreshment, the God who watches over us does not fall asleep; "he shall neither slumber nor sleep," says Psalm 121. "The Lord shall watch over your going out and your coming in, from this time forth for evermore." God the shepherd is watching over you.

God is not only the shepherd of the living, but of the dead. In a few minutes we will turn to the casket and ask our merciful Savior to acknowledge N. as a sheep of Christ's own fold, a lamb of Christ's own flock, a sinner of the good shepherd's redeeming.

For, as it is written in the revelation of John:

The Lamb at the center of the throne will be their shepherd, and he will guide them to springs of the water of life, and God will wipe away every tear from their eyes .... They will hunger no more, and thirst no more; the sun will not strike them, nor any scorching heat.

78

Christ the good shepherd shelters and guides his own.

Jesus' credentials for being the Good Shepherd are simple: because he cares for the sheep; because he knows them and they know him; and primarily because he has laid down his life for them by his death on the cross.

In the Gospel of John, verse 7, Jesus says, "I am the door of the sheep. Whoever enters by me will be saved, and will come in and go out and find pasture." Jesus yearns to be your shepherd. Jesus yearns for you to know his voice and be known by him. Jesus the good shepherd invites you to follow him. In verse 16 he adds, "I have other sheep that do not yet belong to the fold. I must also bring them, and they will listen to my voice." Jesus says, don't stand out in the cold; come into the fold. "I have come," he says, "that they may have life, and have it abundantly" (John 10:10).

Christ the good shepherd guides and protects us, watches over us, shelters and leads us. Christ the good shepherd has laid down his life for the sheep.

And now, may the God of peace, the great shepherd of the sheep, by the blood of the everlasting covenant, make you perfect in every good work to do his will, working in you that which is well-pleasing in his sight; through Jesus Christ, to whom be glory for ever and ever. Amen.
(BCP p. 503)

*Also appropriate for the fourth Sunday of Easter (known as Good Shepherd Sunday) and the following week.

A Dwelling Place

A Funeral Homily For
The Season After Pentecost

Psalm 23; 2 Corinthians 4:16—5:9; Psalm 84;
Psalm 27:1, 5-12, 17-18; John 14:1-6
Music: *How Lovely Is Thy Dwelling Place*

> *Almighty God, our Father in heaven, before whom live
> all who die in the Lord: Receive N. into the courts of your
> heavenly dwelling. Let N.'s heart and soul now ring out
> in joy to you, O Lord, the Living God, and the God of
> those who live. This we ask through Christ our Lord.
> Amen.*   (BCP p. 466)

"Receive N. into the courts of your heavenly dwelling."
I think that says everything about why we are gathered here
today. Because we are here today to affirm that to God's
"faithful people, life is changed, not ended; and when our mortal body lies in death, there is prepared for us a dwelling place
eternal in the heavens" (BCP p. 382). We read in the 14th chapter of the Gospel of John, these words of Jesus: "In my
Father's house there are many dwelling places."

We are here today to offer up our prayers that N. be
received into God's dwelling place, and we are here to prepare and pray for ourselves, that we would be received into
the place of God's dwelling.

What do we mean when we say "God's dwelling place"?
What kind of place is it? What happens there?

Scripture has much to say about heaven.

First, it is a place where we do not have to be afraid. Psalm
27 begins, "Whom shall I fear? Of whom shall I be afraid?
One thing only I seek: that I may dwell in the house of the
Lord all the days of my life." To dwell with God is to not
have to be afraid any more.

81

It is also a place of safety. Again, the Psalmist writes: "For in the day of trouble God shall keep me safe; God shall hide me in the secrecy of God's dwelling." And it is a place of joy and happiness: "Therefore I will offer in God's dwelling an oblation [an offering] with sounds of great gladness; I will sing and make music to the Lord."

It is a permanent, not a temporary, dwelling. Paul writes:

For we know that if the earthly tent we live in is destroyed, we have a building from God, a house not made with hands, eternal in the heavens. For in this tent we groan, longing to be clothed with our heavenly dwelling . . . .

This body, this earthly tent, is a temporary shelter. But God's dwelling place is permanent and eternal in the heavens; as Psalm 23 says, "Surely goodness and mercy shall follow me all the days of my life, and I will dwell in the house of the Lord forever." God's dwelling place is a forever place. It is a real place. And it is into that heavenly court that we pray N. will be received.

How are we who remain preparing for that heavenly dwelling place? Do we, as Paul wrote, "groan under our burden, because we wish . . . to be further clothed" with God's dwelling? Even though our outer nature (our body) is wasting away, is our inner nature being renewed day by day . . . are we prepared not for what is temporary, but for what is eternal?

Those who believe and follow our Lord Jesus Christ, at their death, will rejoice to say with the author of Psalm 84:

How lovely is thy dwelling place, O Lord of hosts, to me!
My thirsty soul desires and longs within thy courts to be;
my very heart and flesh cry out; O Living God, for thee!

Beside thine altars, gracious Lord, the swallows
    find a nest;
how happy they who dwell with thee and praise thee
    without rest,
and happy they whose hearts are set upon the pilgrim's
quest.

("How Lovely Is Thy Dwelling Place,"
The Hymnal 1982, 517)

Amen.

Face To Face
A Funeral Homily For The Transfiguration (August 6)*

Job 19:21-27a; 2 Corinthians 4:16—5:9; John 14:1-6
Canticle: *Nunc Dimittis*

Picture, if you will, a small child learning to walk. The parents stand a few yards apart. The first parent directs the child toward the other parent. At first the child looks back to the first parent for encouragement. But at a critical moment near the middle of the journey, the child starts looking ahead to the second parent, puts out his or her hands, and hurries into the welcoming arms (borrowed from Demetrius Dumm in *Flowers in the Desert,* page 95).

Such a critical moment in Christ's journey happened shortly after the feeding of the 5,000 and Peter's confession of Jesus as the Messiah. Jesus had just finished explaining to the disciples that he must suffer, and be rejected, and die, and after three days rise again. But they could not hear it. Peter flat-out argued with him, and Jesus had to say, "Get thee behind me, Satan." Jesus' heart was heavy. His death was imminent; his disciples were so slow to understand. The Gospel of Luke tells us that Jesus went up to a mountain with four of his disciples to pray.

Luke tells us that, as he was praying, two men, Moses and Elijah, appeared and talked with him. The subject of their discourse was Jesus' forthcoming death, his departure, his exodus from this world. But Jesus did not shrink from what lay ahead of him. He did not succumb to the fear of his mortality.

Scripture tells us instead that Jesus was transfigured, literally, metamorphosized, so that his face shone like the sun, and his clothes became white as light.

85

Then a cloud passed over, and a voice was heard from heaven. The voice said: "This is my beloved Son, listen to him!" His approaching death did not change one fact, but rather confirmed it: Jesus was the Messiah, the chosen son of God.

The transfiguration marks that critical moment in Jesus' life when he stopped looking back to his beginnings, and began to face forward to the cross and his death, hurrying forward into the arms that would welcome him at the other end.

Such a critical moment, a transfiguration, occurs in our lives. It is that precarious moment when we no longer look back to our source, to earth, to life, but when our gaze is turned and we look straight into eternity, ready to run and fall into the outstretched arms of the Father who is waiting for us on the other side. It is because of such a moment, which we call death, that we are gathered here today.

What does Jesus' transfiguration have to say about death?

First, death is not the end: "For to God's faithful people, life is changed, not ended" (BCP p. 382). Jesus, on the mountain, underwent a metamorphosis in which his outer appearance was changed: his garments became white and his face shone like the sun. Likewise, dying is a metamorphosis in which our outer appearance is changed, but our inner nature is renewed and lives on.

Paul, in his second letter to the Corinthians, testifies to the ongoing inner life: He writes:

So we do not lose heart. Even though our outer nature
is wasting away, our inner nature is being renewed day
by day.

So for the Christian, life is changed, metamorphosized, but not ended.

Secondly, when the disciples woke up from their sleep, they saw Jesus' glory face to face. For the Christian, death is but the gate of eternal life, and when we wake up, we too will see Jesus' glory face to face. When he has raised us from death by the power of his own resurrection, we shall see him as he is, and we will be changed into his likeness. 1 John 3 says, "When he is revealed, we will be like him, for we will see him as he is." This is what we pray for in the collect for Evening Prayer when we pray: "O God, grant that we may at length fall asleep peacefully in you and wake up in your likeness" (BCP p. 123). Seeing Christ is what will metamorphosize us. That is what the Christian longs for, waits for: "Vouchsafe to bring us by thy grace to see thy glory face to face" ("O Wondrous Type!" *The Hymnal 1982,* 136).

Jesus' transfiguration was a critical moment in his life. Our death is a transfiguration moment: the moment our life is changed by coming face to face with Christ's glory. It is the moment when, like a child learning to take its first steps, we let go of what is behind, and fall forward into the waiting arms of our heavenly Father.

Amen.

*Also appropriate for the Last Sunday after Epiphany

Lift High The Cross
A Funeral Homily For
Holy Cross Day (September 14)

Job 19:21-27a; Psalm 116:1-8, 12-13;
1 Corinthians 15:20-26, 35-38, 42-44, 53-58
Music: *Lift High The Cross*

The death of a loved one is always a difficult and trau-
matic time. As one of our prayers says, at a time such as this,
"Our hearts fail us, we long for that which cannot be, and
there is none to comfort us . . . [for we know] our eyes no
longer will behold the one we love, and our ears no longer will
hear the familiar footsteps" (See J. B. Bernardin, *Burial Services,* page 139).

If we were in a church with a large crucifix of the suffering, crucified Christ hanging down over the altar, I suspect
it would be natural and quite easy for us to kneel down before that crucifix, because it in so many ways reflects what
we hold inside. Grief. Pain. Broken hearts. Fear. Defeat.

There our suffering mingles with the suffering of Christ.
As Charles Winfred Douglas wrote:

> *O Sorrow Deep*
> *Who would not weep*
> *With heartfelt pain and sighing.*
> ("O Sorrow Deep," *The Hymnal 1982,* 173)[1]

And somehow, gazing at a cross of the suffering Christ,
his head hanging, his body limp, wrists and feet nailed to the
cross, blood emerging from his side, we find comfort.

Before the cross in our time of grief, the truth of it all hits
home: The suffering Lord understands our suffering. He shares
our sorrow. He knows our sadness.

89

Recently, Christians around the world celebrated the feast day in the church year known as Holy Cross Day. It is the day set aside to especially remember Jesus' being lifted up upon the cross, to think on the Man of Sorrows who shares our sorrows: "O sacred head, sore wounded, defiled and put to scorn . . ." ("O Sacred Head, Sore Wounded," *The Hymnal 1982,* 169).

That is one part of Holy Cross Day — the crucifix of the suffering Christ. The other side of Holy Cross Day is the triumphant crucifix. Perhaps you have been in a church or a home where a crucifix with a fully clothed and crowned Jesus is present. That is the other side of Holy Cross Day — the cross as a triumphant sign.

As we sing in "Lift High The Cross":

So shall our song of triumph ever be;
Praise to the crucified for victory.
("Lift High The Cross," *The Hymnal 1982, 473)*[2]

What does Christus Victor — the Christ victorious over evil and death — have to say to us today?

First, Christ has trampled down death by death, as the Prayer Book puts it. By his own sacrificial death, Christ has destroyed death. Paul explained it this way to the Christians in Corinth:

Christ has been raised from the dead, the first fruits of those who have died . . . Then comes the end, when he hands over the kingdom to God, after he has destroyed every ruler and every authority and power. For he must reign until he has put all his enemies under his feet. The last enemy to be destroyed is death.

You see, death is not the end. "For as all die in Adam, so all will be made alive in Christ." For God's faithful people, life is *changed*, not ended. In Christ, life is eternal, and love is immortal, and death is only a horizon; and a horizon is nothing but the limit of our sight. Christ the Victor has destroyed death.

Secondly, just as Christ was raised with a new body, so will we be raised. "How are the dead raised? With what kind of body do they come?"

Paul answers: When you plant a seed in the ground, what comes up looks nothing like the original seed. So it is with resurrection in Christ. A physical body is placed into the ground, but it is a spiritual body that is raised. For the perishable body must put on imperishability, and the mortal body must put on immortality.

In this time of N.'s death and burial, look to the Holy Cross. See there the Man of Sorrows who knows our sorrow. See there also the Victorious Christ, the triumphant Christ, trampling down death by death, and raising us up to new life.

Then, as Paul writes, this saying will be fulfilled:

Death has been swallowed up in victory.
Where, O death, is your victory?
Where, O death, is your sting?
The sting of death is sin . . . but thanks be to God,
who gives us the victory through our Lord Jesus Christ.

Amen.

For All The Saints

A Funeral Homily For
The Octave Of All Saints'

Revelation 7:9-17
Music: *For All The Saints*

> *For all the saints, who from their labors rest,*
> *who thee by faith before the world confessed,*
> *thy Name, O Jesus, be for ever blessed.*
> *Alleluia, Alleluia!*
> ("For All The Saints," *The Hymnal 1982,* 287)

For All The Saints

Today we come together to acknowledge the passing of a saint. I say "saint" because according to the New Testament, the word "saint" is used to describe a person who professed faith in the Lord Jesus Christ and who was a member of the Christian community. N. was such a person: a person who professed faith in Christ; a member of the Christian community.

When a saint departs from our midst, there is grief. We come together to share that grief this morning, so that none of us has to bear it alone. But also deep within us wells up an overwhelming gratitude for the privilege of having known a saint. I am among those filled with thanksgiving today ...

We give thanks for the saints of all ages; for those who in times of darkness kept the lamp of faith burning; for those who saw visions of greater truth and dared to declare it; for those whose presence has purified and sanctified this world. We give thanks for the saints of all the ages; we give special thanks today for N. (See J. B. Bernardin, *Burial Services,* page 115).

All Saints' Day takes on a new meaning for us now, because the company of saints on earth is reduced by one today.

So first of all today, we give mighty thanks for having known and loved this saint.

Who From Their Labors Rest

Secondly, we come together to "pray with confidence to God, the Giver of Life, that God will raise N. to perfection in the company of the saints" (BCP p. 466).

It was Jesus Christ himself who said, "Come to me, all you who labor and are heavy laden, and I will give you rest." We pray today for N., that he [she] may rest from his [her] labors and enter into the light of God's eternal Sabbath rest (BCP p. 465).

"Happy from now on," John writes, "are those who die in the Lord. So it is, says the Spirit, for they rest from their labors." But heaven and eternal life is more than just rest and peace.

Listen again to this reading from the Revelations of John which we heard just a few moments ago. Here we have a picture, a painting, if you will, of heaven:

> *After this I looked, and there was a great multitude that no one could count . . . standing before the throne and before the Lamb . . .*
> *and [they] worship him day and night within his temple, and the one who is seated on the throne shall shelter them . . .*
> *They will hunger no more, and thirst no more; the sun will not strike them, nor any scorching heat;*
> *for the Lamb at the center of the throne will be their shepherd,*
> *and he will guide them to springs of water of life, and God will wipe away every tear from their eyes.*

Actually, it sounds to me from this passage of Scripture that the saints are kept quite busy in heaven: worshipping the Lamb, Jesus Christ, night and day!

They are the company of heaven. They are the ones who stand 'round the throne singing "Holy, holy, holy Lord, God of power and might, heaven and earth are full of your glory."

We are privileged to join in their worship every eucharist, when, joining our voices with angels and archangels and with *all the company of heaven,* we forever sing the hymn, "Holy! Holy! Holy!"

O blest communion, fellowship divine! The saints on earth are knit together every eucharist with the saints in heaven!

Who Thee By Faith Before The World Confessed

Thirdly, we come together to strengthen our desire to know those ineffable joys that God has prepared for those who love God.

The death of N. gives us occasion to reflect on our own lives. At every eucharist, the faithful pray: "And at the last day bring us with all your saints into the joy of your eternal kingdom." Are we desirous of sainthood? Are we faithful? What are we confessing before the world? Trust in ourselves? Trust in our wealth? Trust in our talents? Or are we followers of Jesus Christ? In other words, are we in the company of the saints of Jesus Christ, who him by faith before the world confessed?

Jesus invites us today to join the communion of his faithful body, the saints who confess his name and who follow him as Lord.

Will you today join those who "from earth's wide bounds, from ocean's farthest coast, through gates of pearl, stream in the countless host, singing to Father, Son and Holy Ghost, Alleluia, alleluia!" *(The Hymnal 1982,* 287)?

Let us pray:

> *Almighty God, you have knit together your elect in one communion and fellowship in the mystical body of your Son Christ our Lord: Give us grace so to follow your blessed saints in all virtuous and godly living, that we may come to those ineffable joys prepared for those who truly love you; through Jesus Christ our Lord, who with you and the Holy Spirit lives and reigns, one God, in glory everlasting. Amen.*
> (Collect for All Saints' Day, BCP, p. 245).

Come, O Blessed Of My Father
A Funeral Homily For
Christ The King Sunday

John 5:24-27
Anthem: *Christ Is Risen*

This past Sunday in church we celebrated what is known as Christ the King Sunday. Picture it: Christ the King, subjecting all powers and enemies under his feet, reigning as king in heaven following his resurrection, and awaiting his return to earth and the ushering in of eternity. In some churches, it is celebrated as "Eternity" Sunday.

One of the readings appointed for Christ the King Sunday, or Eternity Sunday, is the familiar Gospel passage from the 25th chapter of Matthew.

Christ is sitting on the throne. He looks to his right and says:

> *Come, O blessed of my Father, inherit the kingdom prepared for you from the foundation of the world; for I was hungry and you gave me food. I was thirsty and you gave me drink, I was a stranger and you welcomed me, I was naked and you clothed me. I was sick and you visited me, I was in prison and you came to me.*

And the righteous will say, "Lord, did you make a mistake? When did we do all these things? Why, we never even saw you before. Are you sure about that?"

And the King will answer them: "Truly, I say to you, as you did it to one of the least of these, you did it to me."

Then the King will turn to those on his left and say, "Depart from me, you cursed ... for you gave me no food, no drink, no welcome, no clothes, and no visits."

And they will say, "What do you mean? What are you talking about? We've never even seen you before."

And Jesus will answer them: "Truly, I say to you, as you did it not to one of the least of these, you did it not to me" (Matthew 25:31-46).

On this day, as we gather to give thanks for the life of N. even as we mourn our loss, and in this particular time, Christ the King Sunday takes on new meaning. Suddenly, the Gospel message of life and death, sheep and goats, the righteous and unrighteous, judgment and eternity are real and close at hand. The death of a loved one opens us to looking at our lives and our deaths in ways we haven't before. I want to speak to some of these things today.

First, as we say in the church's statement of faith known as the Apostles' Creed, we believe that Christ is seated at the right hand of the Father. Christ is King by virtue of his resurrection from the dead. He overcame the dark powers of evil and death. He is the Savior of the world, the Redeemer, the Son of God.

And we can go to Christ in confidence that he will comfort us, soothe us, embrace us, as we cast all our care and grief upon him. He who died on the cross and knew pain and sorrow is a refuge and strength for us, a strong tower to all who put their trust in him. He is not dead, but alive, and having overcome the grave and sorrow, Christ yearns to hold us and bind up our wounds.

Secondly, as we heard in the Gospel of John, "The hour is coming, and is now here, when the dead will hear the voice of the Son of God, and those who hear will live ... the Son has authority to execute judgment."

Scripture is clear that one day each of us will stand before Christ the King. We believe, as we say in the Apostles' Creed, that "he will come again to judge the living and the dead." What words will we hear from the King? Will we be among those to whom Jesus says, "You did not feed me or clothe me or visit me?" Or will we be among those to whom Jesus says, "Come, O blessed of my Father."

"Come, O blessed of my Father." Those are the beautiful words of blessing that all who believe in Christ will hear. Jesus says in John chapter 5: "Anyone who hears my word and believes him who sent me has eternal life, and does not come under judgment, but has passed from death to life."

Have you passed from death to life? Have you put your faith and trust in Jesus Christ? If you have not yet turned to Christ to follow him, I invite you to do so today. It is not just the question, "Are you prepared to die?" It is the question, "Are you prepared to live?" Jesus said, "I came that they might have life, and have it to the full."

Christ the King rules in eternal glory and is with us today. He desires to comfort and hold us. He desires to pronounce the blessing upon us: "Come, O blessed of my Father . . .;" and he yearns to live within us and bring us out of death into life.

Let us pray:

Merciful God, Father of our Lord Jesus Christ who is the Resurrection and the Life: Raise us, we humbly pray, from the death of sin to the life of righteousness; that when we depart this life we may rest in him, and at the resurrection receive that blessing which your well-beloved Son shall then pronounce: "Come, O blessed of my Father, receive the kingdom prepared for you from the beginning of the world." Grant this, O merciful Father, through Jesus Christ, our Mediator and Redeemer. Amen. (BCP p. 505)

Yet I Will Rejoice
A Funeral Homily
For Thanksgiving

Habakkuk 3:17-19a

A couple of years ago on a cold, bleak day, I got a phone call from a woman who asked if I was the pastor. "Yes," I said, "what can I do for you?" "Well," she said, "there has been a death." She went on to tell me that her dog, Pepper, had accidentally gotten out of the fenced-in back yard and had been killed by a car. Her children were very upset. She was upset for them, because they were foster care children, and losing a dog brought up all those feelings of abandonment that these children had already known all too often. She asked if I could come over and say come prayers.

A day later we met at the pet cemetery. When all the prayers were said, the mom gave each child a rose and one by one they walked up to the edge of the grave and put a rose on top of the blanket wrapped around Pepper's body. When it came time for little Jack's turn, Jack placed the rose on Pepper and then looked up into the sky, and with tears streaming down his sad face, he cried out, "Thank you, God, for giving us Pepper as long as you did!"

"Thank you, God, for giving us Pepper as long as you did!" Pure gratitude. Pure thanksgiving.

It is Thanksgiving, and the death of our loved one N. may make us feel not very thankful at all this year, but, I suspect, little Jack said it all for us; for we who knew and loved N. can only cry forth on this day the feeling deep down in our hearts: "Thank you, God, for giving us N. as long as you did!"

Thank you for N.'s life. Thank you for N.'s love. Thank you for N.'s gifts. Thank you for N.'s _____. We thank you, God, for giving us N., for as long as you did.

That story reminds me of a passage from Habakkuk, which I think is the ultimate Thanksgiving Week scripture reading. The prophet writes:

Though the fig tree does not blossom, and no fruit is on the vines; though the produce of the olive fails and the fields yield no food; though the flock is cut off from the fold and there is no herd in the stalls, yet I will rejoice in the Lord; I will exult in the God of my salvation. God, the Lord, is my strength. (Habakkuk 3:17-19a)

In other words, though everything that could possibly go wrong has gone wrong, though the fig tree has not blossomed, even though the olive tree has not produced, and although the crops in the field never developed, even though the flock and the herd have suffered and met tragedy, yet I will rejoice. Yet I will rejoice.

Is there not a word of comfort in that for us also today? Even though everything has gone against us, N. has died, and we can never be the same without him [her], even though the worst has happened, yet we will rejoice . . . we will exult in the God of our salvation . . . because God, the Lord, is our strength.

In God we find strength to carry on. In God we find courage to face tomorrow, and the next day, and the next. In God we are able to give thanks, although at times it seems like there isn't much to give thanks for. Today we are here to say to God, "The Lord is our strength, yet we will rejoice; thank you, God, for giving us N. for as long as you did!"

Amen.

Appendix 1
Suggested Scripture Readings For Funerals

From the Old Testament
Ecclesiastes 3:1-11
Isaiah 25:6-9
Isaiah 61:1-3
Job 19:21-27a
Lamentations 3:22-26, 31-33
Wisdom 3:1-5, 9

From the Psalms (first reading)
Psalm 42:1-7
Psalm 46
Psalm 90:1-12
Psalm 121
Psalm 130
Psalm 139:1-17

From the New Testament
1 Corinthians 15:20-26, 35-38, 42-44, 53-58
2 Corinthians 4:16—5:9
1 John 3:1-12
Revelation 7:9-17
Revelation 21:2-7
Romans 6:3-11
Romans 8:14-19, 34-35, 37-39

From the Psalms (second reading)
Psalm 23
Psalm 27:1, 5-12, 17-18
Psalm 106:1-5
Psalm 116:1-8, 12-13

From the Gospel
John 5:24-27
John 6:37-40
John 10:11-16
John 11:21-27
John 14:1-6
Matthew 25:1-13
Matthew 25:31-46

Appendix 2
Texts Of Suggested Canticles

Christ Is Risen From The Dead

Christ is risen from the dead, trampling down death by death, and giving life to those in the tomb.

The Sun of Righteousness is gloriously risen, giving light to those who sat in darkness and in the shadow of death.

The Lord will guide our feet into the way of peace, having taken away the sin of the world.

Christ will open the kingdom to all who believe in his Name, saying, Come, O blessed of my Father; inherit the kingdom prepared for you.

Into paradise may the angels lead you. At your coming may the martyrs receive you, and bring you into the holy city Jerusalem.

Benedictus (The Song Of Zechariah, Luke 1:68-79)

Blessed be the Lord, the God of Israel;
    he has come to his people and set them free.
He has raised up for us a mighty savior,
    born of the house of his servant David.
Through his holy prophets he promised of old,
that he would save us from our enemies,
    from the hands of all who hate us.
He promised to show mercy to our fathers
    and to remember his holy covenant.
This was the oath he swore to our father Abraham,
    to set us free from the hands of our enemies,
Free to worship him without fear,
    holy and righteous in his sight
    all the days of our life.

You, my child, shall be called the prophet of the Most High,
    for you will go before the Lord to prepare his way,
To give the people knowledge of salvation
    by the forgiveness of their sins.
In the tender compassion of our God
    the dawn from on high shall break upon us,
To shine on those who dwell in darkness and the
                    shadow of death,
    and to guide our feet into the way of peace.

Nunc Dimittis (The Song Of Simeon, Luke 2:29-32)

Lord, you now have set your servant free
    to go in peace as you have promised;
For these eyes of mine have seen the Savior,
    whom you have prepared for all the world to see:
A Light to enlighten the nations,
    and the glory of your people Israel.

Pascha Nostrum (Christ Our Passover, 1 Corinthians 5:7-8;
Romans 6:9-11; 1 Corinthians 15:20-22)

Alleluia.
Christ our Passover has been sacrificed for us;
    therefore let us keep the feast,
Not with the old leaven, the leaven of malice and evil,
    but with the unleavened bread of sincerity and truth.
                    Alleluia.

Christ being raised from the dead will never die again;
    death no longer has dominion over him.
The death that he died, he died to sin, once for all;
    but the life he lives, he lives to God.
So also consider yourselves dead to sin,
    and alive to God in Jesus Christ our Lord. Alleluia.

Christ has been raised from the dead,
  the first fruits of those who have fallen asleep.
For since by a man came death,
  by a man has come also the resurrection of the dead.
For as in Adam all die,
  so also in Christ shall all be made alive. Alleluia.